lolajames decided to write this book after going through her trials of financial instability and uncertainty. It was when she decided to change her financial situation around that she really began to research and study everything there was to know about personal finance and how to correct past financial mistakes.

While on this journey she began to see improvement in her credit rating, an increase in her finances, the ability to begin saving for her first home and the opportunity to create an investment portfolio. Due to her high success rate, she decided to offer all that she had learned to help others out of their financial dilemmas. She has helped numerous individuals achieve the happiness and freedom of their definition of financial abundance.

lolajames has been writing on personal finance for over three years and is the Financial Correspondent for Lucy Magazine, writes for numerous personal finance blogs and continues to assist others in achieving financial success!

"I purchased this book for my teenage daughter who was about to venture off to college. It not only helped her understand the importance of money but it really got her to be cautious of what she did with it!"
-Carol Crump, Ann Arbor, MI

"I bought this book because I felt you could never know too much about money secrets, but after reading it I found myself doing a little financial spring cleaning of my own."
-Ashley Bernal, New Orleans, La.

"Simple, Understandable and helpful in many ways."
-Harold Boyd, Hoboken, NJ

"I always come across helpful books but I don't really use them to my advantage. The guide provided with this book helped me to use the information in my own situation. I even found extra money to put towards investments."
-Mary Jackson, Sherman Oaks, Ca.

"HEY! Where'd My Money Go!?!"

the handy dandy book that will show you how to keep YOUR money in YOUR pocket

lolajames

This publication is designed to provide accurate and authoritative
information in regards to the subject matter covered. It is sold with
the understanding that the publisher and author are not engaged in
rendering legal, accounting, or other professional services. If legal
advice or other expert assistance is required, the services of a
competent professional person should be sought.

Library of Congress Cataloging-in-Publication Data:

lolajames
HEY! Where'd My Money Go!?! / lolajames
p. cm.-
ISBN 978-0-557-05108-3

Printed in the United States of America

*For more information on improving your personal finances be
sure to visit my "personal finance" blog at:*

www.lolawrites.net

or you can email me at:

lola@lolawrites.net

To my God, my strength, my faith....
and all those in the pursuit of happiness
Namaste...

Table Of Contents

Money Flows Freely

*"Commitment leads to action. Action brings your dream
closer."*
-Marcia Wieder

There are many opportunities available that can have money
flowing into your account on a continual basis. Throughout
this book, I will offer you a step-by-step guide to creating the
kind of cash flow that will continuously prove profitable to
you. All you need to do is carefully read, follow along and
make a determination to change your way of thinking, so that
you can create a consistent flow of revenue into your bank
account.

This book will teach you how to plant the trees that produce
leaves of money! That way you can have your own money tree.

Did you know that even though America is the richest
country in the world we still have the highest percentage of
people living paycheck to paycheck? A recent study revealed
that about one in every four Americans say they don't have any
spare cash. Most see themselves stuck in a drowning economy
with nothing to do but work hard and, for most, get a second
job. If this view of financial stability stays this way it could
lead to depression, feelings of hopelessness and the
continuance of a cycle that holds back many people from
potential earnings.

That brings me back to this book. Its sole purpose is to touch the lives of those financially stressed and help them to improve their situation and their lives. Here you will find ways to renew your thought process and stir up the soil so that you can grow that money tree that will take you from feelings of frustration to feelings of satisfaction.

It may be that you are looking to make more money or to start a new business or to quit your dead end job, whatever the case may be you have to start by changing how you view money and its association to you. As you will learn in Part One, Your Mind Is Your Money. You have to work towards placing more emphasis on the positive ideas of money rather than the negative ones.

Part Two, Smart Decisions Matter, will teach you the best strategies in using these positive ideas to train your mind in making decisions that will have long term benefits.

A common misconception is that managing your money wisely means that you cannot have any fun now. It is important to realize how much your lack of money management may cost you in the future. However, as you will learn in Part Three, Organize Your Finances, you must *"divert your attention away from the age old anecdote of budgeting your money, this only focuses your attention on what you can not do."*

On average, Americans accumulate unmanageable debt, fail to save for a rainy day and retirement, and make countless other poor financial choices that eventually leave them worse off. Many of those bad decisions are caused by a lack of knowledge.

This book offers a new option that shows how informative decisions and proper planning can lead to financial abundance rather than financial stress.

"HEY! Where'd My Money Go!?!" is designed for those who want out of their current financial dilemma and desire to live a life of wealth and prosperity.

It can be for that one person working hard everyday to afford the simplest of living expenditures to another who has been able to increase their finances but want to go further.

The information in this book will offer dozens of financial pointers and wise decision making tips with an easy to follow step-by-step guide that allows you to track your progress to a stable financial future.

If you are a w-2'd employee, it will provide insights on how you can use your current skill set into becoming the owner of your own business. You will also learn tax strategies that will allow you to spend what you earn and then pay taxes on what's left over, not vice versa, and how to create ventures that will provide continued monthly revenue.

The basis of this process has been used over and over again by those savvy in investments and finances and has a proven track record of success. I have turned it into an easy to follow plan that will have you experiencing that same success. Some people will obtain financial wealth, others will obtain financial awareness and many will obtain both. Your success completely depends on what you do with the information you will receive.

With this book you will learn sure-fire ways that will get you to:

* Change your mindset about money and its availability

* Understand your current financial situation

* Reasonably determine where you would like to be financially

* Make wiser financial choices

* Map out a plan to get to your goals by teaching you how to run your life like a business, take advantage of the tax strategies the wealthy use and let go of the misperceived notion that *"the rich gets richer while the poor gets poorer"*

* Understand that YOU are in control of your prosperity and how much money you can make

"MONEY DOES FLOW FREELY!"

It's about reconditioning your mindset so everything you do is positive. It's difficult when you are used to your old habits, but you CAN recondition yourself. Financial well-being is obtainable for everyone. It's time to start taking your financial situation seriously.

"HEY! Where'd My Money Go!?!" will deliver the message of financial wealth for everyone, giving proven ways and ideas for anyone to follow to get out of living paycheck to paycheck. It touches the w-2'd employees situation, as well as serves as a reminder for the prominent investor. While there is uncertainty about the financial stability of the economy, this book offers you the opportunity to stabilize your finances and create a continuous flow of money into your life. Now couldn't be a better time for you. Decide to take on a positive outlook on your finances and move in the right direction to financial stability!

Part One:
Your Mind Is Your Money

"You can do what you have to do, and sometimes you can do it even better than you think you can."
-Jimmy Carter

Have you ever gotten your paycheck for your week or two weeks of work, only to realize that it is already spent on the many bills that have piled up on the kitchen countertop? To top it all off, the amount that you received this week barely covers 1/3 of the bills due! When I was in this situation, it left me feeling hopeless and frustrated. I would think, *"What can I do now? Should I look for another job? Should I borrow some money that I won't be able to pay back? Should I just forget about it?"* These questions would become so overwhelming that I would just move on and continue to do what I had been doing, because it didn't seem that anything else would work.

That is, until I made a conscious decision to think differently. It's important to know that the creation and achievement of your financial vision is hindered only by your thoughts, not your ability. You can view it this way — you are in your current financial situation because of your belief system and thought process.

These are things you learned from your parents, or grandparents, a mentor or some other authoritative figure whose belief system you respected. However, these beliefs and actions have gotten you into an unsatisfying situation. Therefore, I ask, *"Why not make it better?"* You can start by changing your actions, and by doing this you will change your financial situation.

I am going to be honest with you; there is no easy way to riches. Making money takes proper planning, execution, and effort and many times this means doing things out of your comfort level. We have all heard that old quote, *"If you continue to do what you've always done, you'll continue to get what you've always gotten."* Here you will find ways to renew your thought process, and irrigate the soil for growing that money tree.

The only other item you are going to need besides this book is an empty notebook. In this notebook you are going to plan out your financial destination and map out a direct path to your desires. We are going to call this notebook **"My Wealth Planner"** or **"Wealth"** for short.

1.1 STEP ONE: Write Down Your Views About Money

Here is where we are going to put **"Wealth"** to work. Open the notebook and at the top of Page One write **"My Views About Money"**. Think of your negative thoughts of money and write them down, with a pencil. *"Money doesn't grow on trees," "easy come, easy go," "the rich gets richer while the poor gets poorer," "money is evil," "money only comes every two weeks,"* etc. I can go on and on, but that's what I want you to do.

Write down ALL of the thoughts that pop up in your head when you think of money. It is VERY IMPORTANT that you write these down with a pencil. You will see why as you continue reading. Now, at the bottom of this list, write down the exact opposite of the phrases you wrote at the top, but this time with a pen. *"Money DOES grow on trees", "easy come, easy go, easy come again", "the rich gets richer and the poor becomes rich and stay rich", "money is good", "money comes any day I choose it to come".*

Now this is where it gets exciting! I want you to take one last look at the list you wrote in pencil and then erase it completely. This symbolizes you taking the weight of your old ways off of your shoulders allowing you to run swiftly and effortlessly into the financial future you have always dreamed.

Now you will only see your positive affirmations about money, written permanently in ink. **Read these daily.**

The reason for this exercise is to get you to see your negative beliefs about money. Once you are able to see them written out, the easier it will be to change your negative behavior. This list will prove valuable in so many ways and will be VERY useful throughout your process of creating financial abundance, so be sure to keep it with you at all times.

1.2 Destined For Success

Once you've completely mastered removing your old thoughts and have replaced them with positive money affirmations, the hard part is over! You are now free to create a lifestyle of complete financial abundance and it's just an effort's worth of work away.

However, you really have to continuously look to your destination and never look back. If you continue to hold on to the old beliefs, even in the smallest way, they will cause you to think that changing your financial situation is a stupid idea. They may even evoke a feeling of fear or doubt. This is why you should start now to completely move away from these old habits and to venture into territory that you have never trodden before.

At times, it's going to get difficult; however, you now have to approach these difficulties as if they were a challenge — one that you are destined to win. Do you remember your old thoughts about money? The ones you had written in pencil? Those were your old beliefs. That was the instability from which you will walk away.

Now look at the bottom half of the page — the items written in ink — these are permanent. These are your positive money affirmations. You will read these and recite these daily and, more importantly, whenever doubt or fear or any other negativity arises.

1.3 Do As You Say

You have to be careful of the words you use in your day-to-day conversations. You may not be aware of it, but the everyday words you use can easily turn into your beliefs and, in turn, into your actions. Our words are a way of telling our subconscious what to believe. They are daily affirmations that affect the outcome of our lives. If we continue to talk in a negative way, we are creating the formation of negative things in our lives.

Therefore, from now on, instead of saying you are trying to do something, say you are doing it. *"I'm trying to become financially abundant."* **WRONG**. *"I WILL be financially* *abundant"* **RIGHT**!! Instead of wanting something, say what you are going to get. *"I really want to buy a new house."* **WRONG**. "I WILL buy a new house." **RIGHT**!

Even just saying it once out loud evokes a feeling of happiness and excitement and, more importantly, commitment to whatever it is you want. Positive affirmations are a way of saying "yes" to your goals, a way of saying to yourself, *"I WILL accomplish my goal"*. This is the feeling you want to keep around — a feeling that is going to push you towards your goals — WHATEVER they may be!

1.4 Focus On the Good Things

Now that you are beginning to understand your old beliefs and the way that they have affected you so far, it's now time to redirect your focus. You must change it from wanting to get out of debt, from not being able to do something, from being tired of your dead end job; to focusing on creating a continuous flow of money into your life, to being well equipped to do this, to becoming a part of a better way of making money. You can start by reciting, out loud, the positive statements you wrote down on your list.

In the beginning, it may seem a bit weird and you may feel foolish; but this is where that quote comes back to haunt you!

"If you continue to do what you've always done, you'll continue to get what you've always gotten."

Remember, if you want to move forward, you are going to have to do some things that you are not accustomed to doing. This may seem silly or pointless, but it has been proven that, when you verbalize your beliefs, those very beliefs become reality. Thoughts become words and words become actions; your actions create character, and character is what others see in you. If you want change, you have to create an arena for change to flourish!

1.5 Know Your Destination

It is impossible to get anywhere worthwhile if we don't first decide on a destination and then map out a route. Just like in everyday life we don't simply hop in our car and just drive aimlessly around town. Just as we know where we are going before we even attempt to get dressed, we should know where we want to be financially before we start just saying I want more money. What do you want more money for? How much money would you like to have?

The more detailed and planned out your desired destination is the easier it will be to walk right up to it and achieve your financial goal.

1.6 Write The Vision And Make It Plain

What slows us down? It is the fact that we really don't know where we are going. We have an abundance of hopes and dreams, but they are all scattered about. This leaves us frantically working towards a bunch of ideas, with no direct way of getting there.

We exert energy and begin to feel like our dreams are beyond our reach, when the exact opposite is actually true. Our dreams are right at the end of our well-crafted plan. Therefore, we need to craft a plan, map out our steps and directions, and follow the course.

1.7 STEP TWO: Create A Vision

This is where you have free range to see yourself, wherever and however you want to be. Take a moment. Set this book down and really daydream about the life you want to live, or the amount of money you would like to have. Whatever works for you, this is your dream. When you are done, on Page Two of **"Wealth",** title the page **"My Vision"** and write down every detail of your vision.

Be sure to write it down in a way that will get you back to the same feeling you felt when you first created the vision.

This will help to put you in the place of your destination. It will add a motivation to really achieve the feeling you feel when you think about your vision.

1.8 Start Off Small

Now that you have a clear visual of your destination, it's time to start making progress. This part is going to be a bit of a challenge, but that's what makes it so good. The first steps are the most difficult, but once you are up and running, there will be no stopping you. Remember, you are already well equipped for the race.

As long as you keep **"Wealth"** near, you will always have the positive affirmations and that feeling you get when you envision yourself living out your goals.

It is important that you take baby steps and work on maintaining a positive outlook toward your goals. In order to succeed in anything you do, you have to have a plan, a firm foundation. When the tides of doubt try to come and topple it down, you will stand strong and remain steadfast, and headed in the right direction.

1.9 Your Current Situation Doesn't Matter— Now Is the Time To Start Creating Abundance

Now that you have decided upon your destination, you have to move towards it. In order to do this, you will have to deal with where you are. However, this doesn't mean you have to wait until the time is right or until you clean up your current situation before you start. It's all part of the process. Dealing with your current situation may seem stagnant, but it WILL move you closer to your destination.

In order to change your current situation, you have to not only change how you view your desired destination, but to stop putting off achieving it with excuses like *"I won't be able to do that!"* or *"It'll never happen for me!"*

Of course, there will be times when you feel like you aren't getting anywhere or it was foolish of you to believe you were capable of doing this. However, I'm here to promise you that it worked for me and I am determined to show you how it will work for you.

This isn't just a process I thought up in my head and decided to test out on the next vulnerable person willing to give it a whirl. This process is tried and true. It is the process I used to rebuild my finances. It is the process I used to create my own business and it is the process I continue to use to sustain all that I have created.

There was a time when I was in a financial position with which I was not happy. I wasn't always financially stable. I spent the early part of my adult life trying to figure out what I wanted to do with my life. I was in college, but would change my major every semester until I just got tired of it and decided to sit out for a semester. Well sitting out a semester turned into a year and a year turned into two. It wasn't until I was inundated with bills and student loans and being turned down for every credit card possible that I realized I had to do something about my finances or I would continue in a downward spiral.

It was then when I began researching the Internet day and night reading articles on improving your credit and growing your wealth. I got so interested in the topic and determined to make my situation better that I took all of the knowledge I had gathered from the Internet and created my own little step-by-step guide to making my financial life better. It wasn't easy but with my determination and seeing the progress I was making I kept at it until I had finally reached my financial destination.

During the process, I must admit, I had many doubts and fears about my financial future. I had always grown up with positive affirmations about being the best I could be and being destined for greatness, but there were still times when I would get a little uneasy about my outcome.

It is easy to doubt all of the wonderful positive things you are taught, when you feel like you are in a hopeless situation. I did stay in that place of fear and doubt for a while. However, my desires for a better life didn't let me stay too long. I realized that if anything was to change in my life, I was going to have to be the one to make the changes. This is where I came up with this first part— change your mindset. Little did I know that I was creating a process that would not only drastically change my life, but would grow to change the lives of many other people. With this, I learned that I held the key to open any door I wanted to have opened.

1.10 You Determine Your Outcome

Now that you have decided to venture out on a journey that will have a remarkable effect on your life, it is important that you recognize that the boat cannot continue to sail without the wind of your beliefs and efforts. If you feel that you need inspiration, include some really good cheerleaders who would love to see you succeed, such as friends and family members you know will always push you forward until you've reached your goal. It's not always going to be easy, but it's not always going to be hard. Use the resources around you for motivation, whether they are a group of friends, or the credit card debt that keeps building up or whatever else you can use to push you out of your situation and into your destination. Use it to your advantage and commit to your vision!

Part Two: Smart Decisions Matter

"A wise man makes his own decisions, an ignorant man follows public opinion."
-Chinese Proverbs

What outside effects makes us choose certain decisions? What makes us think more about each decision that we make? Whether it's in our finances or lives, how do we always know that the decision is based with wisdom? This leads us to the next part, Smart Decisions Matter.

Now that you have committed to creating a better financial future for yourself, it's time to start really thinking about the types of decisions you've made in the past and how those decisions have and still are affecting you. Observe your decision-making habits and change those that are hazardous or harmful. Every decision you make should be a calculated move that will put you closer to your destination.

This is where you will plant the seeds of abundance. In our finances, it's a lot easier to judge the smarter decision. It is easier to see that when we decide not to buy something we really don't need so that we can invest that same amount of money into something that will create wealth would be the best decision.

Even though emotionally we might want the jewelry, or house or whatever else it may be we know the best decision would be the investment. However, this is where a lot of us fall short. Even though we know what's right we, most of the time, still give in to the "right now" and buy the unnecessary item instead, forgetting all about our vision.

As we train our minds to make smart decisions, the process of making better choices will become easier and we will be on a more stable road to financial abundance and planting the seeds needed for growing our money tree.

2.1 Decisions, Decisions, Decisions

Everyday of our lives we are faced with decisions. Some are minor ones, should we wear the black shoes or the brown shoes? Others are major, should I invest in this opportunity or which house should I buy? Either way every decision we make has a profound effect on the type of life we live. If we chose the black shoes and are confident in our choice, we in turn receive compliments on our attire and we continue on with our lives feeling a little bit better about ourselves. Simple.

However, the affects of the major decisions aren't that simple. If you choose the wrong investment you face loosing all of your money or having it tied up in a venture that is not beneficial to you. If you choose the wrong house, it could prove to be costly in the end. Therefore, while the minor decisions affect our lives in some way the major decisions have more importance on determining our quality of life.

Wherever we are in life in the present is solely based on the decisions we made in the past. What career path we decided on, where we decided to live, at what age we decided to have children, how many children we decided to have, what business venture we decided to take, the investments we decided to invest in, how much energy we have decided to exert into our talents, all of these decisions lead us to different places in our lives and determines the type of life we live.

Smart decision-making holds a high place in determining where we are and where we go in life. Have we always made the best decisions? Probably not! I know I haven't always made great decisions. I had to train myself, as well. Most people make some good decisions and some poor decisions. Think about the poor decisions that you've made.

What would your life be like if you had decided differently? What if you were constantly able to make smart decisions? Wouldn't the quality of your life improve?

Decision-making is a skill that can be learned and enhanced. It's a matter of training your mind just as you train your body when you go to the gym.

It's a repetitive step to decide to be conscious of all of the affects your decision will have on you, now and in the future.

Although we haven't always made smart decisions we can learn from the bad ones by making better ones in the future. This is the difference between a good decision and a poor decision. If we find ourselves in a place where we have to make a decision we have made before and we decide to do the same thing we did in the past, even though we know what's going to happen, this is poor decision making.

A lot of the time we get caught up in not wanting to deal with the challenge or pain the smart decision will bring, however it is important to know that, in the majority of cases, instant gratification is usually a sign of long term regret. If we train our minds to see past the present and into the future we can drastically improve our quality of life. In many instances, we are not taught the proper decision making process. In most instances, we don't even realize there is a decision making process. There is and all it takes is the knowledge that it exists and a willingness to learn.

The majority of smart decision-making is based on learning from your old mistakes. Smart decisions are the ones where you choose to do things differently than what you've done in the past.

Whether it's not letting fear keep you from starting your own business this time or using your extra money to invest rather than shop. Changing what you've done in the past to achieve better results for the future, that's smart decision making. There is a saying that wisdom is applied knowledge, so what good are your past mistakes if you don't apply them to future gain? When you forge past your old decision making habits and use them, as examples of what not to do you will be well on your way to smart decision-making.

2.2 Decision Making

This part can get a little tricky and may seem like information overload, but once you have a full understanding of each category it will help you to understand the decision making process a lot better.

There are many types of decisions that will come along, however the majority of them will fit into one of these three categories.

2.2.1 The Most Common Decision Types

There's the "yes/no decision", "options decision", and "only if decision". Let's start with the "yes/no decision". This one is easy. It's where you are faced with a question that requires a yes or no answer. Should I invest? This type of decision is based solely on one of two answers, yes or no. Then there's the "options decision". This decision requires you to choose from many options. Which investment should I put money into? Should it be the one I read about or the one my friend just invested in?

Lastly there's the "only if decision". This one is a decision that you would make *only if* something else happens. I will invest *only if* I can make a twenty percent return. It's important to know the difference between the three major types of decisions we will face. However, it's just as important to recognize the different tactics we use when making them.

2.2.2 The Way We Make Decisions

A lot of the time, we tend to make a decision based on how we feel before we have gathered any information that will help us to make a calculated choice. Or we may base our decisions off of what our mentors have done or what we think we are supposed to do. These are a few ways we make decisions which can prove to be costly or profitable.

The most important thing to remember is there is no one certain way to make a decision. It should all be based on your desired destination and you should seek out as much information as possible. The more we learn about the different parts of decision making the easier it will be to make decisions that will be the most beneficial.

The ways we make decisions will vary from time to time and some are least likely to get you where you want to be than others. For instance, when you use intuition in making your decision you are pretty much throwing your chances to the wind and choosing to let the outcome be out of your control. I understand the term "go with your gut feeling", and have even used it in the past, however this isn't a decision making option I would recommend.

It doesn't allow you to educate yourself on the outcome and is a lazy way of making a decision due to the lack of effort exerted.

Another way we make decisions is through patterns. We continue to make decisions the way we always have. The way we were taught by our parents or through habit. This way only leads us in a circle and keeps us from ever seeing change or advancement. Finally, there's the logical way we make decisions. This is where we weigh our options, view the pros and cons and make sure that we are going to get our desired result. This is the way we want to train our minds to make decisions. It is an educated approach that allows us to almost determine the outcome.

Smart decision-making is all about making good judgments. If ever you are at a point of not knowing why you are about to make a decision be sure to take a minute to stop and evaluate it. Analyze the type of decision it is and then choose to logically make the decision by assessing the pros and cons and selecting the answer that gives you long term success. This should open up some thought and keep you from feeling the effects that will come if you simply choose to emotionally decide.

For some the smart decision-making process will cause feelings of fear or uncertainty. Due to the old conditioning and poor decision habits that we are used to taking, a step onto new ground may seem daunting and may cause some concern.

The more personal the decision; the harder it will become to make a wise decision. The harder it will be to choose a challenging one over one that will bring some kind of instant happiness. In these types of situations we tend to slip out of objective thinking which keeps us from thinking clearly.

2.3 Overcoming Fear And Uncertainty

With anything in our personal lives, we tend to be sentimental and overly cautious. Therefore, it may seem risky for us to make a smart decision. We would rather take the easy route and opt for what we "feel" would be better. If ever you find yourself emotionally tied to a decision take a moment and use a few of these pointers to get you back to objective thinking.

Be honest

It's challenging to take on a new way of thinking. This is especially true when you have been thinking your old way for so long. Old habits are easy to fall back on when you are fearful about what to do next or the decision is an important one. In this case you should step back and ask yourself *"what is it that is worrying me? Is it the outcome? Is it the idea of trying something new? Is it being unfamiliar with this type of decision?"* Whatever it is write it down so that you can really understand what could be keeping you from making the best decision.

Expect A Challenge

Just because we have made a wise decision it doesn't mean there won't be bumps in the road. That's why it's always important to know that in the space between the decisions being made and the outcome, you may begin to worry. However, it makes it easier if you are already prepared for the unexpected.

Stay Positive

If and when feelings of doubt arise try reading your positive affirmations from Page One in **"Wealth"** or the notes about your vision, all of these are tools that will help you past fear and worry and stay on track towards what you have already planned for yourself. It's important to push through the challenge instead of allowing it to be a roadblock. Use your apprehension to help you become stronger in the face of adversity. Turn it into a growth opportunity instead!

Stay Focused

Make it a point to stay committed to success no matter what. Stay clear as to what may be bothering you and address the problem head on rather than giving into it. When you stay strong and focused on the end result all of the worries or fear won't be enough to stop you.

Ignore The Negativity Of Others

Once you have put in valiant effort towards making a smart decision it is important to stay true to yourself and ignore the negativity of others. Keep your vision, stay true to yourself and your decision and disregard the expectations of those around you.

What's important is that you made a decision that is appropriate to get you to where you want to be. Others are only on the outside looking in.

Many times feelings of uncertainty come about due to our inexperience in what we are doing. The way your old ways of making decisions have become habit is through repetition. However, the way to training your mind for smart decision-making will be repetition but also through trial and error. Instead of repeating the same mistake that resulted in an undesirable outcome you have to choose to do it differently. Choosing to do it differently not only shows your desire to make smart decisions, but it will also get you closer to your dreams.

2.4 Knowing What To Decide

There is a lot of talk about our desired destination and keeping that as first priority when we are making a decision. We have even visualized ourselves there and written down notes that will enable us to get there whenever we need a positive uplifting. All of this is pertinent in wise decision-making. There is also a method you can use to guide you along.

When making a smart decision it is critical to know your ultimate goal, being as detailed as possible in regards to the problem to be solved or the decision to be made. This is a crucial first step! Take plenty of time to think things through carefully. In real estate it is called due diligence. Step back and take a good look at everything surrounding the decision.

How would you advise someone else about this decision? What would your advice to them be? Can you make a decision to follow your own advice? These are good questions to ask yourself before making a decision. We tend to make better decisions for others than we do for ourselves, because we are unemotionally attached.

Outside of these questions, we need to not only be clear and detailed about our ultimate goal, but also the long-term impact our decision will have on achievement. For instance, deciding on whether or not to have that ice cream isn't just about breaking your diet it's about the affect it will have on you attempting to compete in your first triathlon.

That one time of giving in to temptation could result to another time resulting in a failed attempt to achieve your dreams. Whereas the lasting affect of not giving into temptation and strengthening your discipline will provide a much better long-term result than the initial desire to give in.

Another example would be a friend of mine who was initially deciding between an older fixer upper house and a new townhouse.

In stepping back and assessing all of the details, he saw that there were many decisions to be made before the decision of which house to purchase. The first decision would have been whether to rent or to buy. Did he really want to live in the town the home was in? Was he going to stay on the career path or at the job he had chosen at this point?

All of these things would be smart decisions that need to be made before he decided on whether or not to buy the older fixer upper house or the new townhouse.

After all of those things are decided then the decision to be made between the two homes would be next. Is it going to be financially wise to have a fixer upper? Which will need more money? Will the difference in the older home and fixing it up be more beneficial than the high cost of the new townhome?

The key to making a smart decision is to be more detailed in regards to everything that will be affected by that decision.

2.5 Know What You Want

In order to have a detailed view, you have to know what's important to you. A key point in smart decision-making is to know who you are and what you want. The reason a lot of decisions we make fall through or never produce the desired outcome are due to our uncertainty in what we really want.

You are the guide to your destination. Wherever you want to go you can go. However, when the destination or outcome you want is constantly changing this leaves room for your decision to not produce to its full capability.

It takes clarity. You have to be clear about what you want. This will not only help you make a strong decision, but it will make it easier for you to put trust in your decision. A helpful way to start towards being clear about what you want would be to list your values.

2.5.1 STEP THREE: What's Important To You

The objective here is to get you to visually see what you consider to be significant. On the Third Page in **"Wealth"** title it **"Values"**. Values are what are important to you. On this page under **"Values"** list what holds precedence in your life. List them in the order of importance. It could be financial abundance, family, commitment, courage, or power whatever means a lot to you list it on this page. This list determines your objectives. The order in which you labeled your values is the order in which you should strive toward each one. Now that you have written out what you really want be sure that the decisions you make are the ones that will put you closer to achieving your values. When you are conscious of your values and have them set in stone making smart decisions become that much easier.

2.6 Research The Facts

Now that you know what's important to you, it's now time to research the facts and determine an outcome. What do you need to know about the problem to be solved or the decision to be made that will allow you to make a smart decision? What would a good decision look like to you? This is a two-step process. First decide what information is important. What do you need to know about the decision to be able to make it successful? How do you make it successful? Is it in your hands? Is it something you can research and do? Research the facts. Do your due diligence.

Next you want to determine the outcome that would make you happy. What do you want out of this decision? What does this decision look like in the end for you? Be clear about your desired end result.

Make sure that the choice you are making meets and eliminates any issues that may arise. Work backwards from your goal. You've researched the facts. Now determine the outcome.

Another detail you want to look into would be the alternatives. The more alternatives you have the easier it will be to see the many directions your decisions could lead you. It's always good to have many views on one decision before deciding on which one works best for you. The more you have to choose from the better.

You should really take your time and look at the decision from all angles. What will happen if you decided this way? How will the outcome be affected if you chose to do this rather than that? Ask yourself as many questions about the decision as you can think of?

You can even ask others what they would do just to get other views on the decision. Use all of this as tools to help you make your decision. After you have dissected the decision it's now time to look at the risk. This is where you want to think of all the risk involved in your decision. It requires organization. Don't try to do it in your head. Write it down on paper. Use a pen and analyze the options. Write down all the pros and all the cons. Look at them very carefully. Do the cons outweigh the pros? Are the pros more important to you? Assess your risk accordingly. Evaluate the consequences of failure. Will it be life changing? Use this risk factor in evaluating the options.

2.7 Be Careful What You Think

Our minds have a lot of control over what we do. This is why we must pay attention to our thoughts and how we let them affect our decisions. On Page One of **"Wealth"**, we diminished our negative thoughts about money and replaced them with positive affirmations. However, it shouldn't stop there. We should continue to take all negative views concerning every aspect of our lives and in this case every "value" in our life and turn them into positive views. Whenever we find ourselves in a position of leaning on the negative views to make a decision we should choose to make it at a later time when we are able to think clearly and be mindful of the outcome not our emotions. If you don't do this all of the information you have gained so far will be wasted.

A favorable approach to careful thinking is to stay observant. Always observe what thoughts you are letting into your mind. What thoughts you are considering when making decisions. There may be some times when we may lean more to making a decision based on assumptions. These are things we just think are right because we have thought that way for so long. Things that we have done no research on we just assume. For example, you shouldn't just decide to quit your job and take on real estate investing because you *assume* every body that does it is making money. There may be some doing well and many others that haven't done so well. This is a perfect example as to why you shouldn't solely make a decision based on assumptions.

If you find yourself basing a decision on an assumption stop and make sure that assumption is accurate. If it is not then you should throw it out and use other facts to help you make your decision.

At other times we may find ourselves making a decision in favor of something or against something because of our beliefs or opinions on the subject matter. We are all entitled to our different beliefs and opinions, however it would be wise for you to think about putting these aside when making a decision because many times they can hinder you from thinking clearly and objectively.

Stress can also be a factor in keeping us from making the best decision. It can have a negative effect on our thinking, take away our concentration from other pertinent facts and hinder us from seeing all of our options.

Therefore, if you find yourself in a stressful situation it is better to wait until it's over before you make any decisions. All of these can hinder us from making clear and smart decisions and they should be taken seriously. If ever you find yourself using any of these thoughts or habits be sure to take a moment and reconsider.

2.8 Practice Makes Perfect

Now that you have become familiar with the types of decisions there are, the way we make them and what keeps us from making smart ones, it's time to put it all into motion and move closer towards your goal. Its one thing to gain a lot of knowledge on a subject, but it's another to actually use it.

Here is a mini exercise you can use to start to put the decision-making tools you have learned to the test. This is just to get you in the habit of being aware of the small everyday decisions you are making and how they effect you long term. It's as simple as asking yourself four questions before making any decision.

1. Is this a necessity?
2. Will I have to stop living if I don't get it?
3. Will this purchase or decision help me get to my destination?
4. Have I given this decision any thought?

If you answered no to any or all of the questions then you should be saying no to whatever it is you are deciding on. Begin by using this process with the easier decisions, such as, when you are going shopping, or looking for the latest power tool or flat screen television.

This will get you to be more conscious of your decision making habits and also train your mind to thinking more about the decision before you make it rather than just going off of emotion.

Once you have conquered being more aware of decision making, you can start applying all of the decision-making pointers to assist you in making smarter decisions that will benefit you.

2.8.1 STEP FOUR: An Outline To Wise Decision Making

I do recommend that you rewrite this outline on Page Four of **"Wealth"**.

Rewriting it helps you to begin to memorize the material so that it becomes like second nature to you. I have just outlined what we've been talking about so that you can see it in a step-by-step process and use it accordingly. Once you get the hang of it you can tailor the outline to fit your specific needs or even develop your own method of smart decision-making.

Smart Decision Making Outline

UNDERSTANDING THE DECISION

Step One: What Type Of Decision Is it?

    1. Yes/no Decision

    2. Options Decision

    3. Only If Decision

Step Two: The Ways Decisions Are Made

    1. Intuition (No)

    2. Pattern (No)

    3. Logical (Yes)

Step Three: Why Am I Making This Decision?

Step Four: Is Something Worrying Me About This Decision?

Why Am I Worried Or Afraid?, Be Honest, Expect A Challenge, Stay Positive, Stay Focused

MAKING THE DECISION

Step Five: Be Clear About What To Decide

Step Six: Know What Kind Of Result You Want

Step Seven: Research the facts

Values, Set Your Criteria, Develop Alternatives, Assess The Risk

NOW ALL THAT'S LEFT IS TO COMMIT!!

2.9 Take The Good

Smart decision-making is simply lessons learned and training ourselves to make sure we evaluate everything that's involved in the process. We must make a conscious decision to make a smart decision. Be sure to stay on track by identifying the decision. Recognize the values the decision supports. You want to make sure it is in order with your ultimate goal. Take time to think about the decision for a while. Learn everything you can about it. Gather as much information as possible.

There will be times when you are unable to gain everything there is to know. In this case make the best decision you can with the information you were able to collect. Other times will present you with a limited timeframe.

Understand this and research as much as you can until it is time to formulate a decision. As time permits continue to think about the decision that's at hand. List as many options as you can, making each one clear and precise. The more you have the easier it will be to make a smart decision.

Alongside listing options set criteria. Use these criteria to eliminate certain options that are shaky or hold no real value. If there is an option that doesn't fit into your criteria or wouldn't be able to add to your desired outcome do away with it.

If you find that your decision isn't going the way as planned simply adjust it so that it does. There are times when good decisions may end up having bad outcomes.

However, you are in control of it all so if you see it not going as planned reevaluate, adapt and move on. On top of this WRITE IT ALL OUT!!! Don't just go over it in your head. It would be impossible for you to be able to correctly analyze everything that will lead you to a smart decision. Use a pen and paper, use the extra sheets you will have left over in **"Wealth"**, so that you can see everything in writing and do away with what doesn't work.

2.10 Leave The Bad

With all of the information you have gained through trial and error, life's experiences and all that has been given to you so far, its time to say goodbye to the days of old consistency and move onto happiness and abundance. It all starts with the decision to leave bad habits behind.

Decision-making plays a vital part in all areas of our life; therefore we must correctly implement the process. At a time when we are receiving new information it is important to not get over zealous. You have learned a lot, but you are not yet a pro at applying it, because simply put, you haven't had the experience. The more and more opportunities you have at applying the decision-making tools, the more you will quickly grow from novice to expert.

Therefore, before you go diving into decision-making it's still a good idea to take it step by step. It's one thing to have confidence in your decision but it's another to think you know it all. Be sure to not skip over the fact-collecting step due to your overconfidence in yourself. Missing this step could prove critical to your desired outcome.

Even though there may be many people whom you consider to be experts on the decision you are making always dissect that persons reasons for formulating their opinion. It could be that there situation is different from yours or the outcome they wanted has nothing to do with what you would like to get. You can seek the advice of experts, however always be sure to compare their approach and their reasoning to yours.

Once again beware of making decisions based on emotions or when you are stressed. When you are overwhelmed with feelings, especially those that are strenuous, you are unable to make clear decisions. If ever you find yourself submerged in your feelings wait until they subside before you attempt to make a decision.

If you can choose a time frame before making a decision be sure to allow yourself enough time to complete the whole process. It's very rare when you are able to have all the time you will need to get as detailed as you can with making your decision.

Therefore, if the opportunity to choose your time limit presents itself take as much as you need to gather everything you need.

Most importantly don't attempt to look at the decision as one whole. Break it down according to your options, criteria, values, outcome and whatever else is important. A decision is multidimensional and should be treated as such. Use the Smart Decision Making Outline and the many other tools provided to assist you in deciding wisely.

Lastly, follow through. Make it a habit to stand by your decision and see it through until you have reached your desired outcome. Deciding on something is one thing but putting your plan into motion so that you see the results is another.

It may seem as though a lot of the information is repetitive or detailed. Or you may be coming up with your own ideals and practices. This is all fine. Just know that these methods are just to be sure you are provided with everything there is to know in making wise decisions.

Once you train your mind with the correct decision making habits it all will come together and you will be able to use your own way of wise decision-making.

2.11 COMMIT, COMMIT, COMMIT

You've done your homework. You have as much information as you would like. You've outlined and analyzed all of your available options and chosen your desired outcome. All that's left is to make the decision and commit to it. Commitment is vital. My mother always told me to make a decision, evaluate the outcome and COMMIT. If it was the wrong decision, learn from it and make a better one. Don't be afraid to make a decision and follow through. If there is uncertainty or doubt there is a weak link somewhere in your decision. This means you should go back and reevaluate your choices and not set a decision until all fear and doubt have disappeared.

When you know you have done all you can and have made the right decision, you will then be able to stand strong and firmly commit. You have all of the tools necessary in making very wise decisions. Now move forward in confident decision-making.

Part Three: Organize Your Finances

"Should you find yourself in a chronically leaking boat, energy devoted to changing vessels is likely to be more productive than energy devoted to patching leaks."
-Warren Buffett

Each one of the parts of this book all work hand in hand. If one part of the process is weak it will cause a domino effect of disappointment and shortcomings. That's why it's important to strengthen every part of the process by applying it to everything you do. Be sure your positive affirmations are strong and undoubted and your vision is clear, detailed and unhindered and most importantly that you are motivated and determined to accomplish what you have set out to achieve. If there is any weak link go back and strengthen it so that you can move forward on a solid foundation.

Once you have rid yourself of your negative views about money, have seen yourself right where you want to be and are prepared to adjust your decision making in accordance with your goals it's time to start watering the seeds for your money tree to grow.

What is important to know here is the misconception of money being scarce and limited is not the reason for our financial shortcomings.

It's the absence of our will power to bring it into our lives that has kept us where we are financially for so long.

A great way to change your current situation is to change how you view your desired destination. Many people have desires for a better financial future, but tend to think that they are too far in debt or they view making more money as hard, if not impossible.

In order to get to better wealth you have to take the *STRUGGLE* out of earning more money and turn it into a challenge. You have to decide to challenge yourself to make it to the exact place you want to be financially. The challenge will not always be fun, but it will motivate you to achieve your goals. We learned in the previous part it's a matter of taking a look at how you've made decisions throughout your life and how those decisions will affect you in the long run. However, now that you have learned how to make wiser decisions, the rest of the process is going to be that much easier. It's now time to get your business in order.

3.1 Before You Begin

Another characteristic of this process is to divert your attention away from the age-old anecdote of budgeting your money. Doing that only focuses your attention on what you cannot do.

Instead make it a goal to know exactly how much you are spending every month. Rather than just spending frivolously make it an effort to be conscious of where your money is going. It's all right to spend your money on the things of your desires BUT if that is what you are going to do then you will have to learn how to create ways to make more money.

The key to financial abundance is to have a constant flow of money circling in and out of your life. And if all you are doing is putting out money then your well of finances will dry up putting you back into a state of financial stress.

Money takes responsibility and activity. Budgeting only fulfills the responsibility side whereas using your money wisely allows you to be responsible with your money by paying attention to how you spend it and allows you to become active in finding ways to create more. With Part Three you are going to focus on your goals and creating opportunities that are going to get you there. It's not about budgeting and penny pinching it's about creating more money to flow into your life.

3.2 Understanding Good Debt Vs. Bad Debt

Before we can begin running a business of prosperity and abundance, we must learn as much as we can about debt and the effects it has on us. Many people think that all debt is bad debt and that it should be avoided at all costs or they should pay it off as fast as they can. This is a common misperception and should be rectified immediately. There are two types of debt. There's good debt and then there's bad debt. Being able to differentiate between the two is what being smarter about your money is all about.

Bad Debt or consumer debt is the debt you acquired to buy things that will eventually lose value. It doesn't have an obvious way of helping your finances. *Good Debt* is debt that's used to buys things that will increase in value over time.

Both play important roles in creating wealth however one is more important than the other. It is imperative to do away with bad debt. *Bad Debt* only takes up more of your money and adds stress and worry leaving you no space to focus on your goals. *Good Debt* has a way of adding to your goals by creating opportunities to create more money.

3.2.1 Good Debt

When you borrow money for something that is going to generate more money for you this will prove beneficial in the end. Therefore, real estate loans, home mortgages or business loans are all sources of *Good Debt*. They will over time create a way to add to your finances rather than take away from them.

Refinancing your home to get rid of the high interest rate on your current home loan is good debt. It saves you money and in some instances will give you some extra cash upfront that you will be able to use for investing or enhancing your home, which may cause it to appreciate in value. Borrowing money for the purchase of a new home is another example of *Good Debt*. Over time your home purchase will produce equity, which in turn adds to your net worth.

Student loans are also considered *Good Debt*. An education affords you the opportunity to obtain a job that will increase your earning potential. They even offer deferments if ever there is a financial circumstance that keeps you from paying accordingly.

Good debt is a way of making your money work for you. If ever you are going to get back more than what you borrowed, you are in good debt.

3.2.2 Bad Debt

When you buy something that instantly loses value it has no benefit to you. If your purchase has no promise of increasing in value it is useless. A lot of our bad debt is obtained by our desires for material things. We may want the newest car or the latest fashion; all of this is acceptable only after we have created a flow of income to sustain our lifestyle. We often overlook the effects of purchasing items with our credit cards. When we use our credit cards for purchases and are not prepared to pay the balance in full before the due date we are actually increasing the cost of our purchase. Every month you make the minimum payment on your credit cards an interest is added to your bill increasing what you originally paid for the item. Therefore if you opened an account with a store for the 10% or so they offer off of your initial purchase you will eventually pay it all back, if not more in interest.

Bad Debt can be tricky; because we cannot physically see the effects it has on our finances. We just see to it that we pay our balances on time so that we don't get a late fee but if you took the time to add up all of the interest that's added on to your balance, it would prove costly and you would be able to see how you are wasting your money.

3.3 When Is It Worth It?

There may be some instances where what we would normally consider to be bad credit can be turned into good credit. For instance, under normal circumstances, a car loan would be considered bad debt because a car will depreciate in value. However, if you are purchasing another car for better gas mileage, this in turn saves you more money in the long run and makes that loan good debt.

The ideal way of creating debt for a home and a car is to try and borrow for a house before your first major car loan. The best type of debt is a mortgage. A home builds value and this value adds to your wealth. If your current circumstance requires you to purchase a car before a home make it a point to not go out and purchase the most expensive car on the lot. Opt for the more affordable car so that you can leave some of your finances open for a future home purchase.

3.4 Debt Management

Debt not only causes stress and worry, but it could also harm your credit rating. If you miss a payment or, in most instances, are more than thirty days late your creditors report this to the credit bureaus. The negative report in turn has a huge impact on your credibility and your credit score.

When deciding whether or not to take on new debt it is important to consider your debt to income ratio. This is the percentage of your monthly gross income that goes toward paying your debts. The key is to keep this number as low as possible. A rule of thumb is to not have your personal debt exceed, an estimated, 36% of your total income. When working on creating wealth you don't want any money to have to go towards unnecessary debt. If you want something that will not increase in value; pay cash for it. If you can't pay cash for it then don't buy it.

Credit cards should only be used in the case of an emergency. If you find yourself having to use your credit card a lot, slow down on your spending, allocate a plan to bring the balance to zero and discontinue the use of your credit card. Incessant spending is a form of mismanaging your money. This is what puts most of us in debt.

3.4.1 Misperceptions About Getting Out Of Debt

There are many substantial ways to getting out of debt. However, there are some common ways of getting out of debt that are not as advantageous as we tend to think.

Bankruptcy

This seems like the easiest answer because once it's done a lot of your debt is erased. However, this is where your wise decision skills should come into play. While considering bankruptcy, think about the long-term effect it will have. Now that have you have decided to create financial abundance there is going to be a time when you are able to pay off your debt and take part in many advantageous opportunities. If you file bankruptcy this will stay on your credit for years and that will hinder you from being able to take part in those opportunities.

Remember to always look at the long term effect of your decisions rather than choosing instant gratification and consult the advice of a well researched attorney if you feel the desire to learn more about your current financial situation as it relates to bankruptcy.

Debt Consolidating Companies

A lot of these companies put you on a program where they total up the sum of all your debt and arrange an "affordable" monthly payment. However, in most cases, that "affordable" monthly payment is only paying the interest and doesn't even touch the principle balances you owe. It would be better to contact your creditors on your own and negotiate a repayment plan that lowers the remaining balance and also does away with the interest rate. It may take some time but anything is negotiable.

Credit Repair Companies

There are a lot of reputable companies to choose from but there are a lot of unreliable companies that perform illegal ways of removing negative items from your credit. When deciding on a credit repair company be sure to do your due diligence and get as many references as possible.

Transfer Funds

There's the method of transferring the balance from a higher interest card to a lower interest card to save money. This is profitable only if it is done wisely. It is one thing to use the lower interest card to pay off the balance on your higher interest card, however it is not wise to make it a cycle. Once you have transferred the balance from the high interest credit card to the lower interest don't go and run up the balance on the high interest card again. This only creates a pattern of instability and continuous bad debt.

More Loans

Just as with transferring funds, refinancing your home to consolidate your debt can yield great results. This can happen only if it is done right the first time. After you have paid down your debt and gotten control of it it's not wise to go out creating more debt for yourself. When you do this you are not only putting yourself in the same position by doing the same things but you are also wasting the equity you worked so hard to build in your home. Therefore, if you are going to refinance your home to pay off your debt do just that and be responsible enough to not incur anymore.

3.4.2 Getting Out Of Debt

It's important to know that debt takes longer to get out of than it did to get into. It also takes more discipline, dedication and focus. Once you create a plan to get out of debt, you have to stick to it or else you will find yourself in a vicious cycle of unwanted bills. You have to look at it as running your life like a business and one of the first steps to a successful business is to dissolve all bad debts.

3.4.3 STEP FIVE: Debt Elimination Plan

1. List Your Debt.

On Page Five of **"Wealth"** make a list of all of your debtors. Include the interest rate, total balance and minimum monthly payments.

2. Put Debt In Order

With a visual of all of your debt and their terms you can now make a plan to pay them off. Put the debt with the highest interest rate first and list the rest accordingly. This is the order in which you are going to pay them off.

3. Set Aside A Certain Payment

Now that you know the order in which you are going to pay off your debtors, you should set a specific amount to pay on each one. In order to get any progress you are going to have to pay more than the minimum payment. The key here is to put a serious dent in the balance due so that you can move on to the next debt. It would be wise and prove beneficial if you would aim to pay at least $150 more than the minimum amount due. So that's what we will commit to. This will give you a greater progression towards a zero balance.

4. Payments

While you are paying the minimum plus extra on your first debt, you will continue to make the minimum payments on all of your other debts. However, once you have paid off your first debt, you will take whatever the amount of that payment was and add the minimum payment of the next debt to be paid off. For instance, if the payments for your first debt were $200, $50 minimum payment and $150 extra, and the next debt to be paid has a minimum payment of $150 you will pay $350 monthly on the next debt, the $150 minimum payment and the $200 from the previous debt. This may seem next to impossible however in order to make some progress you will have to sacrifice.

3.5 It's An Obligation

The idea of sending so much money monthly may make you a little apprehensive in the beginning, however once you really commit and make a few payments the progress you see will make you feel a lot better. It may even make you want to pay more and more. The feeling of getting closer and closer to being debt free is liberating. It takes away a lot of stress allowing you to focus your energy on more important matters.

Remember even though you have set up a plan towards eliminating debt, it is adjustable. You should always be looking for extra money that you can use towards debt elimination. If you find that you have incurred an unnecessary expense or feel like you wouldn't mind giving up a leisure activity for a short period of time to allow yourself to get out of debt faster go right ahead. The quicker you get out debt the better your chances of achieving financial abundance.

3.6 Moving Towards More Detail

Another way to be certain you are making your money work for you is to take a detailed look at your spending and expenses. You've written out your vision and now it's time to map out how you are going to get there. In order to realistically achieve your financial goals you have to know where you are in comparison to where you would like to be. When defining your current situation it is imperative that you're honest and detailed. Write out all of your monthly expenses, including the payments you will be making to eliminate your debt. This is considered your "base".

Anything you blow off or leave out will only hinder you from reaching your goals. So be sure to check and recheck everything you write out in regards to your base. After you have written out everything concerning your base the next things you are going to write out are where you would like to be financially, or your "goals". This can be anything from buying your first home to having a certain amount of money in savings to getting a certain amount of return on your investments. Any and everything you desire to do or have should be written down as your goals.

3.6.1 STEP SIX: Roadmap To The Future

Now that you have a clear understanding of what to write down under your Base and your Goals. It's time to add the details. At the top of Page Six in **"Wealth"**, write the word BASE.

Under BASE you are going to write:

Your monthly income before taxes

Your monthly expenses

Your assets (home equity, mutual funds, savings etc.)

Your liabilities (credit card debt, mortgages, loan balances etc.) Anything else you can think of (have you written down EVERYTHING you bring in and take out? Everything you own and owe?)

After you've written down everything, do not judge your situation or become fearful or unmotivated. Your current situation is not the real concern. Where you are going is your only concern. Now that you know where you are its time to determine where you are going.

Now at the top of Page Seven write the word GOALS.

Under GOALS you are going to list:

Any and every financial goal you desire

3.7 Setting A Time Frame

I recommend allowing yourself a reasonable amount of time to achieve your goals. Ideally you could set a 3-month timeframe to get you "headed" toward your GOALS. And then allow yourself at least a year to accomplish them. You want to create a plan that will give you results immediately, this will keep you motivated, as well as a plan that is realistic, one that will keep you from disappointment.

3.8 Creating The Flow

With your BASE, your GOALS and a reasonable timeframe in place, it's now time to move forward. You now want to create a flow that will continually feed into your plan allowing you to accomplish your GOALS. Here is where you will plan out how you are going to spend your money and focus on creating a continuous flow of more money in and less money out.

The first step is to keep a monthly chart of how much you are spending and what you are spending it on. This is where honesty comes back into to play. Every month be sure to write down everything you bought, every bill you paid, etc. A great tool to use that will help you with accuracy is to keep ALL receipts and maybe even purchase a software program. I use Quicken; however there are many options available that will help you keep track of your spending.

Once you have your spending habits written out before you, it will be easier for you to readjust them so that you are headed in the right direction. It's not just enough to write down your spending habits. You want to dissect the amount you are spending and what you are spending it on. Take time to look over the list. Is there any amount that strikes you as too big? If so this is a red flag of overspending. In this instance it would be a good idea to cut down spending in that area. Its good to use your money-spending chart to see how much money you can actually free up.

I'm certain you have heard this many times over and over again, but keeping track of your spending is a very helpful tool. When you are able to see what you are spending you are able to see the amount of money you are throwing away by overspending and this helps you to move toward better spending habits.

You have to develop a healthy relationship with money and see it as your way to freedom. Once you see your frivolous spending habits as a hindrance to reaching your ultimate goal you will soon learn to respect your money and even become cautious of what you spend it on. You will notice, as you continue to pay attention to your spending, that you will have extra money left over. This is the money you want to put into a separate account that you can use towards investments and debt elimination.

Keeping track of your spending is something you should do every month. Even after you have reached your goals. Without it there is the possibility of going back to overspending. The good thing about your spending chart is nothing is written in stone, therefore once your finances grow you can adjust it in accordance.

3.8.1 STEP SEVEN: Chart Your Spending

Whether you are going to keep your receipts to manually chart your spending or use them to document your spending with computer software designed for money management make it a point to keep accurate records of your spending. In **"Wealth"** on Page Eight write in **BIG BOLD** letters **"REMEMBER TO CHART YOUR SPENDING!!!"** That way every time you refer to **"Wealth"** for guidance or to be sure you are on the right track, Page Eight will serve as a reminder to keep track of your spending.

3.9 Putting Your Plan Into Motion

Another step in calling order to your financial life is to create entities. An entity can range from a corporation to a partnership this includes Limited Liability Corporations (LLC), Sole Proprietorships and the like. The purpose of creating an entity is for the protection of your assets but you should also use it to ignite the spark of an entrepreneurial spirit. This way you can gain the experience of running a business and the opportunity to make more money doing what you enjoy.

Another reason for creating an entity and allocating your money accordingly is the tax advantage that is provided. The most utilized tax system is the one where many people make money, pay taxes on what they've earned and spend what's left. This is an unfair system considering how hard most people work on a day-to-day basis. However, there is a more profitable approach to taxes and those with the knowledge of this system are using it all the time. It is where you make money, spend money and pay taxes on what is left over. The majority of Americans are overpaying on taxes because of their lack of knowledge on how to correctly organize their finances.

3.10 Spend What You Want And Pay Taxes Later

The better you organize your finances the easier it will be to utilize tax strategies that will allow you to keep more of your earnings for yourself. You have to create an entity that will draw in revenue and allow you to write off certain things as an expense.

There are a few options and you should definitely look over your situation and decide which entity best meets your needs.

3.10.1 Limited Liability Corporation

A Limited Liability Corporation, or an LLC, is like a combination of the best parts of a partnership and a corporation. It offers the owners protection from personal liability for any debts the LLC may incur. In this way it is similar to a corporation. It differs from a corporation in the way it is taxed. An LLC doesn't pay it's own taxes it is considered a pass-through tax entity. This means any profits or losses of the LLC passes through to the owners. The owners in turn will report them on their tax returns.

Along with the passing through of any profits or losses, the owners of an LLC are protected from personal liability for any debts the business incurs or any claims filed against the business. In other words, if your LLC is unable to pay a creditor that creditor cannot come after any of your personal possessions. This is where the "limited liability" comes from.

Now even though your personal possessions are protected under the "limited liability" there are some instances where you can become liable. If you yourself directly injure someone, personally guarantee a bank loan, fail to deposit taxes withheld from your employees wages, intentionally perform fraudulent acts that cause harm to the company, use the LLC as an extension of your personal affairs this will cause you to become liable for your actions.

It is very important that, if you choose to form an LLC, you treat it as it's own business and keep it separate from your personal affairs.

Tax Outlook

The key tax advantage of creating an LLC is that you don't have to pay taxes on the money that your business spends. Legitimate expenses to your business can be deducted or "written off" from your business income. This will lower the profits of your business that you have to report to the IRS and in turn decrease the taxes you will be required to pay.

3.10.2 Corporations

A Corporation is a legal entity separate from its owners. Like an LLC, it has liability protection. Therefore your personal assets are separate from that of the Corporation and you aren't held liable for the debts of the company. The difference between Corporations and an LLC is that with Corporations you can raise capital by selling shares of stocks.

There are also some additional responsibilities that are involved with Corporations. For instance, in order to remain a Corporation you must hold an annual meeting and take Corporate minutes and appoint the appropriate officers.

Tax Outlook

Aside from being able to write off the expenses of your business, a Corporation is also an independent tax entity, separate from the owners and anyone who may control and/or manage it. Therefore, the owners will not use their personal tax returns to pay tax on any of the Corporations' profits. The Corporation will pay the taxes on these profits itself. The owners will pay income taxes only on salaries or bonuses received from the Corporation.

3.11 The Benefits Of Entities

Regardless of which formation you decide is best for you, there are advantages in forming an entity.

Personal Asset Protection

Both entities allow your personal affairs to be separate from the companies. This leaves you free and clear from any debts or claims incurred by the company.

Professional Appearance

The appearance of Inc. or LLC after your business name can add authority and convey an image of seriousness and dependability. This will make a potential customer feel comfortable in doing business with you.

Name Protection

In the majority of states, no other business can form a Corporation or LLC using the same name of your Corporation or LLC.

Deductions

Normal business expenses can be used as deductions from the profits of the company allowing for a decrease in taxes.

The key to running your life like a business is developing a financial strategy by organizing your finances the way businesses are organized.

3.12 An Organized Financial Life

Allocating your funds accordingly so that you know when you are profiting and when there is a loss is important to achieving financial abundance. When your finances are organized it makes it clear to see where you are and make the proper adjustments to get to where you would like to go.

Part Four: Create A Continuous Flow Of Money

"I like thinking big. If you're going to be thinking anything, you might as well think big."
-Donald Trump

With your finances in order, you can now have a clearer view of the extra money you have available as well as ways to spend less and create more money that you can use for investments. It's now time to create ways to make your money work for you. The majority of the time we are advised to put our money into a savings account and collect the small amount of interest that it pays yearly. This method gets us nowhere, fast.

If you want to accelerate your way to financial wealth you have to take non-traditional steps. It's all right to include stocks, bonds and mutual funds into the mix of your investment portfolio. However, you also want to take a look at a wider range of options. It would be wise to look further into these opportunities and choose those that provide continuous cash flow. Choose those, which will water your seed of prosperity so you can watch it grow rather than letting it dry up and wither away.

With every venture you take on, you should definitely consult with someone who is knowledgeable and can offer the pros and the cons of whatever it is you are deciding on getting involved. The knowledge they can offer you will reduce your risk being that you will have a seasoned advisor who will be able to help you decide which opportunities best fit your investment needs.

A great idea when deciding what type of investments to choose for your investment portfolio is to first create standard rules that you will follow. You should base these rules on how you would like your portfolio to perform for you; the kind of results you want to achieve. This gives you a guideline to follow when different opportunities come your way.

A good recommendation is to include real estate in the mix; these provide a high rate of cash flow as well as tax benefits. A misperception to disregard is that the only way you can gain an enormous amount of wealth is from real estate investing alone. This is untrue. While real estate can provide a great amount of cash flow there are other ventures that can add to the return on your investment and add to incoming revenue. A recommended read would be Gary W. Eldred, PhD "The Beginner's Guide To Real Estate Investing" to gain valuable information on Real Estate Investing so that you can better understand the logistics and the process involved in adding Real Estate Investments to your portfolio. You can find this book in many bookstores or at Amazon.com.

When it comes to knowledgeable investing the potential for creating a continuous cash flow is limitless. Whether you are just beginning or already have a performing portfolio, there is plenty of opportunity to create greater cash flow.

If you feel as though you may not have enough money to start investing you are wrong! All it takes is a small amount of cash and consistency. Many wealthy investors started out investing very little money but they were consistent year after year until their cash flow grew larger and larger. Successful investing is a process. It's a matter of working with what you have, learning what works for you, sticking with it and being flexible enough to accept or decline certain opportunities that will enhance the performance of your portfolio. It's about investing in opportunities that will in turn create more opportunities.

4.1 The Way Money Works

It's better to always remember that money attracts more money and more money attracts more opportunities. Therefore, if every time you make a profit from one of your investments and you use it in a way that will not bring you anymore profit you have simply wasted your previous efforts of obtaining that money in the first place.

Here's an example, let's say you work hard for a solid month straight saving every penny you could so that you could use it for, after careful research, an investment opportunity which you find to be very lucrative. Now the end of the month has come and you invest everything you worked so hard for into this opportunity. A couple of months go by and you find that your earnings from your investment have doubled. So you take which you have earned and go out celebrating until every penny is gone. Get where I'm going here? Exactly!! What you have done here is taken your earnings and spent them on things that cannot bring you any more money. You pretty much threw your entire months work and the opportunity to gain more money to a night of celebration and fun.

Now I'm not saying you have to hold tight to every penny you receive from investments but I am saying you should think wisely about what you do with your profits rather than just blowing them off.

A better way of utilizing those earnings would have been to leave what you initially invested in the opportunity there and take the profits from your investment and research another investment opportunity.

That way you are creating ways for more money to come into your life. Remember money attracts money. Therefore, if you spend all of your earnings you leave nothing for money to be attracted to however if you use it wisely in money creating ventures it will come back to you over and over again. It will also afford you the opportunity at more than just one night of celebrating. If you continue to work in this manner you can very well find yourself in a position to have all that your heart desires.

4.2 Follow The Leader

A great way to get started in any arena you are not familiar or comfortable is to seek out the path of those that are successful in that area. Read about certain things they did or how they paved a way for themselves. Were they trailblazers? Did they follow a certain pattern? Did they stay inside the box? Really take a moment to learn of those well accomplished in the field.

After ample research choose whichever one is similar to you in personality. Which one responded in a way you would. Or did things the way you do them now. Once you have narrowed your search down you can use this person as a mentor until you find someone.

Find out what types of investments they were apart of. How did they get started? What are they doing now? All of this can help you in your efforts to becoming a successful investor.

4.3 System Overload

Now I know what you are probably thinking and in some ways I can agree. From the introduction until now you have been provided with a load of information that has probably got your head spinning and wondering if this wealth stuff is really for you. Well I'm here to take on the role of one of those cheerleaders Part One told you to go out and get an tell you:

You can do it!!!

It is going to take some time, it is going to take some research and it is going to take A LOT of effort and discipline on your end. Think about how worth it it's going to be on the other side of financial stress, enjoying everything your hard work has gotten you. In fact, once you arrive on the other side what you feel is hard work now will seem so easy compared to the benefits you will have.

Becoming financially stable isn't an easy feat. The many people who you see enjoying riches are enjoying the works of their hard labor and dedication to achieving their goal. It happened for them and it will happen for you. Just put your mind to it, focus in on the prize and charge after it with all of your might and you will reap a great harvest grown from your seeds of stamina.

4.4 Starting The Cycle

Now back to our regularly scheduled program. So how might you get started in investing? Well, after you have found your "pseudo" mentor, you would next start to prepare for the investment opportunities you will find through research and word of mouth.

4.4.1 Don't Wait

It is a common misconception that before you start investing you must pay off all of your debt first. This isn't the correct way of creating wealth and may sometimes even act as an excuse for you to not get out of your financial rut. You still want to stick with the plan you previously created for getting out of debt however you DO NOT have to wait until you are debt free before you start investing. Actually investing while still keeping your debt free plan will prove valuable because you will be able to use the extra income you've created from your investments to pay off your debt which will make it easier and faster to get out of debt rather than just with your set salaried income.

4.4.2 Create An Account

To begin, you want to start thinking about a monthly amount you can commit to have taken from your earnings, aside from the amount you are using to pay off your debt. This is what many of the wealthy call paying yourself first. This means you allocate a certain amount to be taken out of your paycheck and put aside for investing.

It does not mean setting aside a certain amount for leisure activities. It will be used for creating more income through investments.

Once you have that amount set in stone open a savings account at your bank and discipline yourself so that you put that amount in the bank at the end or beginning of each month. Once you have reached a nice balance you can now start researching investment opportunities that will create more income.

4.4.3 Reinvest

As with the lesson you learned in the previous paragraphs, you now want to reinvest any income you gain from your first investment into other opportunities that will create even more income. This will start your cycle of successful investing and also give you the chance to invest in bigger and better opportunities that will offer higher profits.

Staying disciplined in this cycle will have your money working for you. This will also leave you with the opportunity to focus on finding more and more income increasing investments.

4.4.4 Guidance

Having a knowledgeable set of people on your side offering you all of the advice they possibly can is another important attribute to add to your journey. Even though you have your "pseudo mentor" and have read up on their strategies it is always that much better to have someone who is knowledgeable to answer your questions and even refer investment opportunities to you. Lawyers, accountants and anyone else used to dealing in investments can all prove to be valuable. They can help you with anything from creating your investment plan, to implementing it, and most importantly sustaining it. I'm certain you've heard it said that it's better to surround yourself with people that are smarter than you. This allows for you to always be in an environment to learn new ideals and ways of doing things.

4.5 Investments Breakdown

You've been disciplined in building a substantial amount of money in your investment account but may still be feeling a little nervous about how to use that money. This is where you have to trust your research and those you have sought out for advice. With all of that in place you can decipher your investment opportunities against what they provide and if what they have to offer is what you are looking for.

4.5.1 Flexibility

You should know that you do not have to focus on just one type of investment. Actually you will find that you will have a lot more to gain if you have many different types of investments in your portfolio. That's the key to an over performing portfolio, the willingness to be flexible and diversify your investments. You should dissect opportunities in many different arenas that may have the ability to provide you with strong returns.

4.5.2 Research

Now that you have chosen to change your situation this makes you responsible for every action you take. That means you can no longer walk away from an opportunity simply because you don't know enough about it. It's now time to research any and every opportunity that is presented to you so that you thoroughly understand it's benefits and it's shortcomings. You can no longer allow yourself to just call an investment risky and walk away from it. It is your responsibility to research it and completely understand why others are calling it risky. Your research may prove to you that the only risk in the investment was your not knowing how it works and how it can perform in your portfolio. Therefore, always remember that the more you know about an investment the more you are able to determine if it will work for you.

4.5.3 Use Your Resources

Always remember the team of knowledgeable people you've created. You will find that some know more about an area where you are weak and vice versa. Never overlook those who are within your reach because almost all of the time there will be someone who will be able to provide you with some valuable insight.

4.5.4 Look At The Benefits

As with any type of investing or money matters, you have an individualized goal you would like to reach. A certain objective you have in mind. Because of this you want to make sure to pay attention to the benefits you will be receiving from the particular investment and then decide if it lines up with what you are expecting.

It may be that you just want to build up your net worth or you may want to have a certain amount of cash flow every month. Whatever it is be sure the investment you are researching is able to perform accordingly.

When you stick to your requirements; you will make sure every opportunity you take part in will get you there. It's about choosing the right opportunities for your particular situation rather than jumping at every investment that sounds good.

4.6 Proper Planning

The first thing you want to do before you do anything else is to map out a plan. This is always key in anything you do because it doesn't leave room for indecisiveness. This is the reason I had you write out your vision in Part One and create a Debt Elimination Plan in Part Three. And it's the same reason I am going to have you create an Investment Plan. Once you have a plan written out before you, your only choice should be to do everything possible to see the plan to the end. When creating your Investment Plan all it takes are four steps and answering a few simple questions to get you started.

4.7 STEP EIGHT: Create An Investment Plan

On the top of Page Nine of **"Wealth"** write **"My Investment Plan"** and start with Step One.

Step One: Set Your Goals And Time Frame

It's important to identify your goals and the time period in which you would like to accomplish them. If you are using your portfolio to pay off certain debts decide when you would like to have them paid off. Therefore, use Page Nine to write down your reasons for investing and next to them write down the timeframe in which you would like to achieve the results.

Step Two: How Much Risk Are You Willing To Take?

The answer to this question will be strongly influenced by your income, financial responsibility, as well as how determined you are to reach your goal. The result of this question will vary from situation to situation. There are different risk profile tests that are available on the Internet. Simply use one of the many available search engines to search for "investment risk profile tests". I suggest you take two or three so you can get a thorough perspective of the type of investor you are.

After you've taken the Risk Profile Tests use Page Ten in **"Wealth"** to summarize the type of investor you are and how that relates to the types of investments you should choose.

Step Three: Commit

There's that word again. And guess what?? It's going to keep coming up. As with any plan you have to follow through with it in order to see the results for which you planned. Being committed to your plan will give you a better chance at achievement and building wealth. Usually there would be nothing to write down here but on Page Eleven I'm going to ask you to write down **"I WILL COMMIT TO..."**(and write all of the things you wish to accomplish with your investment portfolio).

Step Four: Start Investing

With Steps One through Three complete it's now time to move forward with your well crafted plan and INVEST!! Use your team of experts and the information you've gained through your research and get started.

4.8 Types Of Investments

A good way to evaluate investments and make sure that what you are investing your money in is beneficial to you is to get a complete understanding of the options that are available. There are a variety of ways you can invest your money, however in choosing which ways are right for you it's important that you know how they perform and how they will be beneficial to you.

Bonds

These are considered fixed-income securities. It most commonly refers to securities that are founded on debt. Therefore, if you were to purchase a bond, you would be lending your money to a company or government. Then the entity you are lending your money to will agree to give you a certain amount of interest on your money as well as pay you back the amount you loaned them.

The great thing about bonds is their relative safety. If you were to buy bonds from a firm entity, your investment is pretty much guaranteed. A downside to bonds are due to their little risk.

Whenever there is little risk there is little return. You can be sure to not hit it big if your portfolio is full of bonds.

If you were determined to be a low risk investor through taking your investment profile tests then bonds would definitely hold a high priority for you.

Stocks

When you purchase stocks in a company you become part owner of the business. This means you get to vote at the shareholders meetings and it also allows you to receive your share of the profits, or dividends, that the company sets aside for its owners.

So in an effort to compare the characteristics of stocks and bonds, you will see that bonds provide a steady stream of income and a peace of mind knowing that your investment is, for the most part, secure whereas with stocks your investment amount and profit will shift with the market. They go up and down in value daily.

With bonds you are almost guaranteed a return on your investment, no matter how small it may be, however when you purchase stocks, there is no guarantee. You will find with some stocks that you won't gain any profit.

The way you make money with stocks is if the value of your stock increases. It has been seen in a lot of cases where this has not happened. Stocks are definitely more riskier than bonds, however if the stock in your said invested company sky rockets you could very well reach your investment goal faster. It's your decision to make. Remember to due your research on the company in which you are choosing to purchase stock.

These would be for a moderately aggressive investor.

Mutual Funds

Mutual Funds are a mixture of stocks and bonds. When you purchase a mutual fund, you are putting your money together with a group of other investors. This gives you the opportunity to obtain a professional manager that will select investments that are right for the group.

Mutual funds are carefully set up with a certain strategy in mind. This strategy could range in anything form large company stocks, to start up business stocks to government bonds and even international ventures.

The number one advantage of purchasing a mutual fund is that you don't need much experience or time in doing so. That's where the professional managers tasks take place. They will do the research and handling of your money. That doesn't mean you get away without doing anything. Your job is to research the mutual fund before you decide to purchase it. Knowing that you chose the right mutual fund for you will allow you to leave the progression of your money in the hands of the manger handling the business of that mutual fund.

It has been said that you can get a greater return on your investment by purchasing mutual funds due to the fact that you are turning your money over to a professional because they are a little wiser in choosing investments.

There are some aspects of mutual funds that you should know about. For instance, mutual funds come with certain fees that can drastically decrease your return. These fees can include the cost in hiring the managing professional, yearly fees and even transaction fees when you purchase or sell your shares in a fund. All of these can definitely add up and become a nuisance to your profits. You should purchase mutual funds with careful consideration and a close look at everything it entails including the fees.

A well-researched mutual fund can be a great addition to the portfolio of a low risk investor up to an aggressive investor.

4.8.1 Alternative Options

You now have a little more insight on the two main categories of securities available to you, which are stocks and bonds. Many investments will fall under one of these categories. However, there are many other alternatives that can create profit as well. Understanding these will prove to be a little more complicated than the previously discussed investing strategies. These are generally higher in risk but usually will yield a high profit.

They are usually not recommended if you are just starting out in investing, because they require specialized knowledge. Therefore, if you are not completely certain about these investments you should definitely consult an expert who is proficient with these types or you could find yourself losing a lot of money. You definitely don't want or need to jump into the deep end of investing. You can build a strong financial foundation with the basics and then move forward to the more aggressive opportunities when you are ready.

Real Estate

There's a lot of talk about real estate investing and wealth. I have even talked about it briefly in this chapter. There is also a misconception that anyone who gets into real estate can be on their way to becoming the next Donald Trump. This is a misperception that you should definitely steer clear of if you want to prosper in the world of real estate investing. It is not a happen over night venture and it definitely is not a venture that assures great wealth for everyone who enters. As with anything else, real estate investing takes a lot of planning and studying. Although it can be very profitable, there are many pit falls that can happen. However, the more you learn the less likely you are to fall.

If planned properly, real estate investing can provide a continuous cash flow almost immediately. However, you can't get it by going out and buying every cheap house you come across. It's strategic planning. The same type of planning you did for creating financial stability and an overachieving portfolio. That's the same type of planning you will have to do for creating lucrative real estate revenue. It would be very wise to have a group of real estate investment pro's on your side before you venture into this investment strategy.

Options

These are a privilege to buy or sell. One person sells options to another person. This gives the buyer the right to buy or sell the particular security at a price and time agreed upon by both parties. There are two types of options, calls and puts.

Call

A call gives the buyer of a particular option the right to *buy* an asset, which usually ends up being stocks at a specific price within a specific period of time. The buyer purchases the option hoping that the stock will greatly increase before their option expires. If this happens the buyer can then can buy and quickly resell a certain amount of stock that is usually specified in the contract or they can be paid the difference in the stock price when they decide to exercise the option.

Put

A put gives the buyer of the option the right to *sell* an asset, which is usually a stock, at a certain price within a specific period of time. Those who purchase puts are hoping that the price of the stock will drop before the option expires. This will give them the opportunity to sell it at a price higher than its current market value and gain a great profit.

Options are definitely more intricate than your average stocks and bonds and that is why it is for the time when you become more advanced in picking and choosing your investments.

Futures

Futures are contracts on commodities, currencies, and stock market indexes. It is an attempt to predict the value of these securities at some date in the future. Hence, it's name. They are very high risk due to the heavy dependency on speculation. A positive attribute of Futures is that they are often times used to lock in on a specific price for future purchase therefore if the locked in price is cheaper than what it currently costs a profit is gained.

FOREX

FOREX is a term used for the Foreign Exchange Market. It is a cash market where currencies of nations are traded. Often times the trading occurs through a hired broker. Foreign currencies are continuously bought and sold across local and global markets and investments can increase or decrease in value based upon currency movements. The market conditions can change at any time as a result of current events. The goal of investors in FOREX trading is to profit from the rising up in value of whatever type of currency they have purchased.

These are just a glance at the many investment opportunities that are out there. As stated before there are a wide range of investments and strategies you can take part.

You will find many that are just right for you and those that are not good for your situation once you start really researching and looking for purchases to add to your portfolio. An investment plan's different objectives may require different investment strategies. All of these are ways to keep you informed on investing and decide what is best for you. For specific investment advice, you should consult a Financial Advisor. We will talk more about Financial Advisor's and their role in you financial future in Part Five.

4.9 Determining A Lucrative Investment

A really good way to measure how well an investment will do is to look at it's past performance. Let's take mutual funds for example. If you come across a fund that has been making 10% a year for the last 20 years, you could conclude that this fund will continue to perform this way. You should never quickly invest in something that you "think" or it "sounds like" it has the potential to make money. If it hasn't proven itself to you then you should wait until it does.

During your investing you are definite to come across scams that will sound like a good idea. In this case it is important to not act on your gut reaction.

It's OK to listen to the opportunity, but have patience, read up on it, research it's track record and even consult with your experts before making any type of decision.

4.10 Where Do I Find These Investments?

A lot of investors find good investments through research, reading, and word of mouth but mostly from a broker or Financial Advisor. They are knowledgeable in understanding the types of investments that are good for assisting you in creating a portfolio that will perform to your expectations. Financial Advisors are also good at informing you of very useful tax benefits.

It's okay to do this, but listen with a filter. Ask your self why is this person trying to get me to invest in this certain company, mutual fund or annuity. Is the person going to make a higher commission because you buy into that product as opposed to another one? Does this person own any shares in that investment?

In order to not get scammed, you have to have a basic understanding of the different types of investments that are out there, about how well they compare to other investments, and what type of tax deferred accounts are available.

Unfortunately, this is going to take some work. It's a lot easier just to put your trust in someone else, but that is the best way to lose all of your money and fast. Only invest in something when you understand it and believe it will make you money.

4.11 Diversifying Your Portfolio

In this area it is wise to follow those who have gone before you and not just invest in one thing. You should choose multiple opportunities to take part. Some options could be oil and gas, your own business or an already existing business, stocks and real estate. As far as the exact name of the examples above, that is for you to research and decide. There are no set types of investments and there definitely aren't "cookie cutter" plans to follow. People's vision of the performance of their portfolio is different. Therefore, it is your duty to seek out investment opportunities and decide which ones are right for you. Growing wealth is a process. The more you learn the more your wealth grows. You should make it a point to envision the desired profit you wish to receive from your portfolio then learn everything about all of the opportunities that will get you there.

Don't forget the people you sought out along the way who may possess the knowledge you need to educate yourself more. Use all of your resources. No ones ever acquired wealth on their own accord. It's always been with the help of others and the many books, magazines, newspapers and television programs that are available.

Research will not only get you headed in the right direction comfortably, but it will also take some of the risk out of the opportunities. A few tips to remember are:

Learn The Market

I can't focus enough on research and educating yourself. When you become knowledgeable of certain aspects it makes it easier to determine where certain opportunities are headed and if they are a good fit for your portfolio.

Pick and Choose

Once you have decided the outcome you would like to see and you know which investments will get you there focus only on these types of investments. The more narrowed down your search the easier it is to focus and really learn as much as you can.

Watch The Numbers

Take time out to calculate the profits of each investment opportunity and the length of time it will take to obtain them. It's always better to see the numbers written out rather than estimating them in your head.

Stick To The Plan

Always follow the plan you've created. This is your map to your desired destination. If an opportunity arises that is hyped up by a friend or colleague always take a moment to make sure it fits into YOUR plan. Don't simply jump in based on the emotion and excitement of someone else. What's good for them may not be good for you.

There will be times when you will encounter uneasiness or feel uncertain about your entire plan. In this case it is best to not make any decisions and wait until those feelings pass over. They will pass over and you will be extremely happy that you waited to make decisions after the feelings of doubt passed rather than making a decision in haste with a clouded mind.

4.12 Active vs. Passive

A common decision often over looked by many people interested in investing is whether or not they want to be an active investor or a passive investor. Now this isn't to say that an active investor is one that takes part in choosing which investment to put their money into. If this were the case, I would strongly recommend we all take on the active investor role. However, the role of an active investor is a little different from that. If you were to take on the role of an active investor this means, if you were to invest in a business, you would most likely take on some of the duties of management. The same goes for other ventures, as well. If you choose to be an active investor you would have to contribute some kind of time and devotion to the daily operations of that venture.

A passive investor is more like a silent partner. You would put up the money and other people would be responsible for running the operation. With passive investing there may be times where you run the risk of becoming lackadaisical and not pay too much attention with the progress of your investment. This is something you want to avoid. Just because you are not a part of the daily operations of the venture you should still be very involved with its progress and growth.

Value Investing

Alongside being a certain type of investor comes your type of investing. The type of investing you are susceptible to will depend on the goals that were determined in your investment plan. There are three main types. One would be Value Investing the other being Income Investing and the last one being Growth Investing.

Value investing entails looking for stock that is selling at a price for less than the value of their associated business. This is where you would look for stocks of businesses that you feel are undervalued. A Value Investors' strong belief is that the stock market exaggerates when hearing news regarding the economy or any other causes that effect the stock market.

This overreaction causes a change in the price of the stock that may not really represent the value of the business. If a well-researched execution is in place this allows for the Value Investor to purchase underpriced stocks that will prove to be very profitable. However, there is risk in Value Investing because everything is still, to a certain degree, speculative.

When determining what you think a business is worth there are a few ways you can research the stock in which you are interested. You can look at the present earnings or use research to determine future growth and cash flow. The way you decide to choose the stock for which you would like to purchase is solely up to you. It is recommended that you leave room for error when buying the stock at a discount. This will allow for a cushion just in case the amount you estimated the business to be worth is slightly higher than it's determined worth.

Income Investing

Income Investors are interested in high dividends. What this means is that they are looking for companies that have a lot of cash but couldn't find any investment opportunities to invest in therefore they "return" the surplus of cash to it's shareholders (high dividends). By doing this it allows the Income Investor to create a continuous flow of income.

The types of companies that Income Investors usually prefer are more established companies. The companies that are at full growth potential. They no longer have the need to reinvest their earnings into themselves and therefore can pay out their earnings to their shareholders.

The foundation of Income Investing is to find a well-established company that will pay out high dividends allowing you to create a large sum of continuous income over the long term.

Growth Investing

Lastly there's Growth Investing. This type of investor looks for companies that they feel are growing or will grow quickly. These are normally new businesses that are becoming popular amongst their targeted consumer.

Growth Investing and Value Investing are constantly compared as well as thought to be completely opposite of each other. They are both based entirely on what you speculate after you have done your research. It's just a matter of what you are comfortable with. If you choose to step away from popular opinion then you would probably like the idea of Value Investing where you can purchase the stock of a company you think has been undervalued. If you prefer to choose a company that you see as profitable in the future then your path would be with Growth Investing. It's all a matter of preference.

4.13 IRA's

While we are talking about investing and creating lucrative Investment Portfolio's let's take a quick look at IRA's, what they are, why they are important and their role in your portfolio.

An IRA is an Individual Retirement Account and, as the name suggests, is a way of saving for retirement. It can also provide some tax advantages. There are quite a few types of

IRA's. Your employer can provide them or they can be self-provided. Some types are:

Roth IRA

With this IRA you would put money into this account with funds that have already been taxed. This usually means if you needed to withdraw money from it that money would be tax-free. All transactions completed within the IRA don't have any tax effects.

Traditional IRA

The funding for this type of IRA is, most of the time, tax-deductible because the money that is deposited into the fund has not been taxed yet. As with the Roth IRA any transactions regarding this type of IRS have no tax effects. However, any money withdrawn from this account is taxed.

SEP IRA

This is sort of an "exception to the rule" type of IRA. With an SEP IRA an employer can deposit money into a Traditional IRA rather than to the normal pension fund account that would be in the company's name. This type of IRA is usually utilized by small businesses or people who are self employed.

Simple IRA

This type of IRA is similar to a 401(k) plan as it allows the employer and employee to deposit funds into the account. However, there isn't a certain amount that you have to deposit.

Self-Directed IRA

The Self-Directed IRA allows you to make investments with the funds in the account.

With a Traditional IRA the money used to fund it comes from your income before it is taxed therefore the tax advantage here is that you get to subtract that amount from your gross income before your taxes. This will lower the amount of taxes you are subject to pay.

Here is an example. Let's say your gross income for 2008 is $70,000 and you used $5,000 to start an IRA. When it comes time to do your taxes you would only tax an income of $65,000. Another tax advantage of a Traditional IRA is that any increase in your account is tax deferred until you start to withdraw money.

A Roth IRA offers a different type of tax advantage. It doesn't give you immediate tax relief because the money you fund it with was already taxed. However, when you decide to begin withdrawing money from the account this money IS tax-free because you already paid taxes on it.

It is important to set aside extra money for your retirement as long as you don't limit yourself to a certain amount of money. Use your IRA to be an addition to the wealth you are creating through your investment ventures.

4.14 Getting What You Want

Now that you've had a briefing on the different characteristics of investment opportunities, the different characteristics of you, the investor, and the different types of investing it's now time to set forth on a journey of getting what you want. You know you can't get to a place you haven't really determined. Therefore, you must decide what you want from your investments and the timeframe for which you want to receive it. In that case, keep **"Wealth"** near and use Pages Nine, Ten and Eleven handy when implementing your Investment Plan.

As mentioned earlier, if you want to build your net worth the amount of liquid cash wouldn't really matter. You would probably be more focused on the performance of certain investments and the amount of the return on your investment. However, if you were choosing to invest because you want to have added income then you would be more pleased with an investment that provides a monthly cash flow.

All of these decisions must be made before you even start researching investment opportunities. The same way you took a moment to vision your life the way you want it you should've taken a moment to visualize the desired results you wish to receive from your investments. You should've asked yourself why am I investing in the first place? Make sure every opportunity you invest your money into is in line with your answer to that question. Always do your research and move cautiously with the advice of your group of experts and your choices to guide you. The more you get your feet wet the easier it will be in deciding which ventures are right for you. There is a lot to the world of investing, but there is also a lot to gain from it. Anyone is capable of investing and creating extra income from their investments. It just takes time, effort, research and that ever present word in this book COMMITMENT!!

Part Five: Take Control Of Your Wealth

"Innovation distinguishes between a leader and a follower."
-Steve Jobs

With the wealth of knowledge you have gained from this book and your own research, you will be well on your way to achieving your financial goals. Actually implementing your plan will keep you aware of your finances and when they are headed in the right or wrong direction.

Considering the extreme discipline that is required in achieving your goals you should definitely be concerned with having total control of your finances. This doesn't mean to do it all yourself. It does mean to be completely involved in your finances and not simply trusting someone to do it for you.

It is important to have the assistance and guidance of those who may be more informed in a certain area however it wouldn't be a wise decision to allow someone to have complete control of your finances and the decisions that go along with them. All the knowledge that you have acquired along the way will help you to take and keep control of your own financial matters.

You want to be able to care for your trees after you have created a forest of wealth. You don't want to allow someone to just go chopping down your forest of wealth after you have worked so diligently in planting, watering and growing it.

5.1 Building Your Circle

One of the key players in your team of wealth should be your Financial Advisor. Their role is to assist you with your finances. This can be done through helping you with investments, providing you with investment opportunities, as well as making sure any other matters pertaining to your money are in order.

I've decided to dedicate a great deal of this chapter talking about Financial Advisors and their role in your financial stability. While I do feel it is great to have Financial Advisors on your team, I am also very adamant about you being aware of everything that is going on with your finances and why certain things are being done with your money. With that said here are a few recommendations for choosing a Financial Advisor that is going to be a perfect fit for you.

5.2 Steps For Choosing A Financial Advisor

The initial meeting with your potential Financial Advisor is more like an interview for both parties. This is where you both will ask questions accordingly to see if you can continue a progressive relationship that everyone will enjoy. As you go into the interview, you should take the following questions along with you.

You should also take a moment to think of any other questions you may have. You should have a firm grip on what you want from the Financial Advisor. Take the time to explain your financial goals to them. This will allow them to decide if they are capable of helping you achieve them.

After you have given them the opportunity to know you it will be easier to move on to learning about them, their credentials, their strengths and weaknesses and so on.

Step One: Experience

You always want to know how long a person has been practicing their craft. It shouldn't be the determining factor in if you are going to hire them or not. However, it will help you in assessing their eligibility (it can also serve as a great tool when negotiating a fee).

Alongside the depth of their experience, you also want to find out the types of clientele they are used to working with. Do they mainly work with big corporations, small start-ups, experienced individuals or those new to the investment world?

After you have asked them about their experience, as it relates to your situation, allow the Advisor to explain their experience and approach to you. Remember, if you are just starting out, an Advisor that is willing to offer you financial advice and counseling would be most beneficial to you.

Step Two: Qualifications

Any person can say they're a financial expert. You should ask the Advisor of their qualifications. Some validation to them calling themselves this would be if they are recognized as a Certified Financial Planner or even if they are a Certified Public Accountant or Certified Personal Financial Specialist. All of these certifications are offered to individuals who are proven knowledgeable in the field of financial planning. If the Advisor mentions any type of certification you should check their background by contacting the professional organization with which they belong. You can also ask the Advisor why they feel they are qualified to offer financial advice.

Ask the Advisor what tools and steps they use in staying current with the changing market. You want someone who is flexible enough to stay on top of changes. Remember to be as thorough as possible. You want to get as much information as you can to help you with making an educated decision. Keep in mind an Advisor that has proven knowledge in tax, retirement, and estate planning as well as insurance and investments will be valuable in the long run. The more expansive their knowledge the more they can pass on to you.

Step Three: Services

You want to know what you will be getting if you choose this particular Advisor. You can only find this out by asking. Find out everything the Advisor provides to their clients. Is it advice only in specific areas? If so what are these areas? Are they licensed to sell mutual funds or stocks?

In most circumstances, Financial Advisors cannot sell insurance or securities without securing the correct license. They must also be registered with the correct association in order to give investment advice. It is your job to get this information from the Advisor and then validate it through research.

If you are not sure where to find the information simply ask the Advisor they should be more than willing to give you this information. If they are not then your decision should be made and you should move on to another Advisor.

If someone is accredited and licensed in their required field they will be more than happy to allow you to research their credentials. After they have given you the direction to go, you should definitely go and check their background. Just because someone is accredited doesn't mean they have always done everything right. It is up to you to check their work ethics alongside their credentials.

You have found out the types of clientele the Advisor possess. Now it's time to find out the types of financial situations the Advisor prefers and their approach to these different types of situations.

It's proven that people tend to give better results when they are doing something they enjoy doing. Therefore, ask the Advisor the type of situation they enjoy working in and see if your situation fits their liking.

Then you can move on to finding out the Advisors approach to certain situations. How will they plan out your financial future? Will they only take part in specific areas and leave you to figure out the rest? What type of views do they have on investing? Are they aggressive? Cautious? Does this fit with your profile? All of this is to be considered with determining if the Advisor is the right fit for your team.

What are there financial limits? Do they only deal with a maximum or minimum amount? Once they recommend an opportunity to you will they follow through in acquiring it? Or will they outsource you to someone else? All of this is important to know and should play a valuable role in your decision.

Step Five: Relationship

The Advisor may be the only person you would have to build a relationship with or they may have assistants that will be handling your situation as well. If this is the case, then you will need to meet with any and every body that will have something to do with your finances. And interview them in the same way you interviewed the Advisor.

If the Advisor does outsource some of there work to other professional outside of the office, you will want to be sure to get their names and numbers, set up meetings with them and research their backgrounds and credentials as well.

It is important to know as much as you can about everyone that will be involved with your finances. You are the leader of your wealth and it is pertinent that you have creditable people assisting you in achieving your goals. If you find that a part of the team your Advisor works with is not reputable enough for you ask them if they are willing to use someone else. Even be able to offer a few references. In the instance they are willing to work with someone you've recommended. Great. If not, you can always move on. The most important person in this process is you. You want to be comfortable with the people you are working with and have a piece of mind that they are doing the right things with your money.

Step Six: Payment

How will you pay for the services rendered by the Advisor?

This should be asked in the interview and is also included in the agreement should you decide to go with any specific Advisor. You should ask the Advisor how they are usually paid. Some Advisors are paid through the company they work for. This means you would pay a fee or a commission to the company and in turn the company will pay a salary to your Advisor. Other Advisors may have an hourly rate, or set fee or even a percentage of the assets you've gained through their efforts and advice.

Another way the Advisor can be paid is through a commission they receive from the product they sell to you. It is calculated by taking a percentage of the amount of money you invest. If this is how the Advisor is paid, ask them the percentage you are required to pay.

Take careful note of this percentage and keep an eye on the recommendations of an Advisor that is paid on commission because sometimes that commission could sway their opinion of a certain investment opportunity. They may recommend a product that works well for them, financially, but not for you. Always be concerned with why anyone is recommending something to you. Even ask them and then move on to doing your necessary research before coming to a conclusion.

One last way the Advisor can get paid is through a combination of both. They may charge a fee for development or consultation and then a commission from anything sold. Some may even subtract a certain percentage of off their set fee if you take any of their recommendations. This is where it gets tricky and you should always remember that you are in control of your wealth. You should never feel pressured to purchase or invest in anything you are not comfortable.

If a recommendation comes from your Advisor and you are uncertain take some time to think about it. Read up on it, ask the opinion of others and draw a conclusion from that. The investment opportunity will be there when you decide. You don't have to hurry up and buy just because it was hyped up. If it happens that you took too long to decide and the opportunity isn't there anymore then maybe it wasn't meant to be. It is better to be able to rest knowing you made the right decision then hurriedly get involved in something that will have you constantly worrying. Take your time. It took time to create the money you are using to invest. Don't just throw it away on an opportunity that someone else think is great.

Step Seven: Estimates

It is certain that an Advisor won't be able to give you exactly what they will charge, you can ask for an estimate. After you have explained to them your situation and your goals they should be able to give you a ballpark figure on what you can expect to pay. Remember this is only an estimate and is not something you can hold the Advisor to.

This is also where you use the Advisors years of experience and your negotiation skills. If they are lacking experience but you still feel they are knowledgeable and able to handle your money accordingly you can negotiate a lower price. However, if you are dealing with someone who has been in the business for years and has a proven track record then you will probably have to pay whatever fees they have set.

Use their fees in determining if it will profit you. If not you may need to look for someone else who is more affordable. However, be sure not to lose experience and knowledge looking for the cheapest Advisor. There are instances where you can find someone who is willing to work with you in regards to payment. However, you will have to pay for quality. Don't short yourself in the long run looking for a cheaper alternative.

Step Eight: Benefits

Who else will be benefitting besides you? The relationships and partnerships the Advisor has created could be beneficial to you but in some minor cases they could harm you. The Advisor may have developed a certain kind of relationship within their circle that will benefit them if they recommend you to someone in their inner circle.

For instance, there may be a lawyer your Advisor use that gives the Advisor a percentage every time they recommend someone to them. This is fine as long as your Advisors judgment isn't altered due to the benefit they will be receiving. It is perfectly normal for these types of relationships to be formed and it can also help you if the Advisor and lawyer are used to working with each other. However, it's just something you want to be aware of so that you can be certain someone is being recommended to you for your best interest and not just the Advisors gain.

Ask the Advisor of these types of relationships or any other conflicts of interest such as any special arrangements they may have with insurance companies or any other companies that sell financial products.

Step Nine: Work Ethics

This may seem obtrusive but you should ask if the Advisor has ever been disciplined for any unethical behavior in dealing with clients. If you don't ask you won't know and the next unethical act could be against you. Even after they have answered you still can continue on and look up their ethical history. There are different professional boards where you can obtain this type of information. The National Association of Securities Dealers, as well as many of your states insurance and securities departments will be able to assist you in researching any disciplinary action that has been imposed on a potential Advisor.

You can even contact the organization the Advisor belongs to, you should have acquired this information in Step Two, to find out of any unethical behavior. There is also a form called Form ADV. This is the form Advisors use to register with the Securities Exchange Commission. There are two parts to this form. Part One gives information about the education and any disciplinary action taken against the Advisor for the last ten years. You can find Part One of an Advisors ADV on the website of the SEC. Part Two gives information about the services and fees associated with a particular Advisor. You can get Part Two from the Advisor.

It is recommended that you ask for the ADV Form Part Two from the Advisor and review Part One on your own when making a decision to choose a certain advisor.

Step Ten: The Agreement

Before you even choose an Advisor ask them to give you everything they discussed with you in writing. Be sure it includes their fees and the details of their services. Keep this with you as a reference to use when making your decision and even after you have chosen an Advisor.

You can use the written agreements you collect from all of the Advisors you interview as a comparison chart and even seek ways of negotiating prices amongst them. Once you look them over you may notice that one Advisor charges less for a certain service than another. Or another Advisor is willing to perform certain services in more detail than the others. Use these to create your own contract that you can present as an offer to the Advisor that best suits your needs.

In the world of finances everything is negotiable. Nothing is set in stone. Of course, a lot of people would like for you to believe that but this isn't the case. If you present a reasonable offer there is room for change.

By performing thorough interviews you will be able to create a relationship with an Advisor that best suits your liking and your financial goals.

All of these steps will help you with getting to know the Advisor better. It will reveal just how involved they are willing to become. You don't want to expect your Financial Advisor to be a teacher and hold your hand through the process. However, you would like their willingness to explain what they are doing and why it is they are doing it. After all in the end it is YOUR money they are doing it with.

The steps are in no particular order. However, you should use all of the answers to the questions to conclude if a particular Financial Advisor is right for you. Sit and think about each interview. How did you feel about the meeting? Did you have a good feeling? Were you comfortable with that person? Do you feel you could get along and move forward with a relationship with this person? Did you feel like they were listening to you and your needs and were genuinely interested in helping you achieve your goals?

This is a long-term relationship you are creating. You don't want to get involved with someone you are not able to trust. Go over the interviews in your head. Sleep on it. Take as much time as you need to come to a solid decision you will be able to stand behind.

5.3 STEP NINE: Choose Your Financial Advisor

On Page Twelve of **"Wealth"** title it **"Financial Advisors"**. Here is where I want you to first research at least three Financial Advisors you feel could assist you, contact them and set up interviews. Write the names, date, time and location of each interview. On Page Thirteen write down all of the questions you would like to ask the advisor when you go in for the interview.

Take **"Wealth"** with you and ask everything in the notebook as well as any other question you may think of during the interview. Be sure to write down any important information from each interview on the extra pages of the notebook. Title each page with the additional information on it after the name of the Advisor. That way once you are done with all of your interviews you can compare your notes from the three interviews.

If you didn't like the first three set up three more interviews and keep doing this until you find an Advisor that is just right for you. Remember it's not a race to the finish line; it's a steady pace to gaining control of your wealth.

5.4 Being Aware

A Financial Advisor is an important component to building your wealth, however the most important part is you. The key to leading your wealth is to be aware of where your money is invested and how it's performing. The more knowledge you gain the better your relationship will grow with your Advisor. You will be able to recommend certain ventures and get their advice on it rather than having the burden of recommendations laying heavily on them. When you feel in control of your money it allows you to make confident decisions about your future.

5.5 Keeping Your Circle Rotating

You've sought out the help of mentors, lawyers, accountants and Financial Advisors and now you must respect their opinions and take everything into consideration.

Always keep the lines of communication open. You've come a long way. The uncertainty about your future is no longer in existence. You are well on your way to achieving the goals you have desired for so long. With your Changed Mindset, you are capable of seeing the change and by learning how to make Smart Decisions you are able to put the change into effect.

Everything is laid out and your path to financial stability is clearer than ever before. Stay on top of all of your affairs and keep your team of motivators and Advisors close at hand.

Life, as you know it, is about to change. That is if it hasn't already. You have everything you need to succeed now all you have to do is continue with motivation and will power to make it to the end.

5.6 Leading Your Circle

Always resolve to know everything that is going on with your finances. Seek out new ventures. Create new ways of making money and always leave room for additional Advisors and mentors. You can't do it alone but you can do it with a team of others who are willing to help you and be helped by you. Keep your finances in order so that you are running your life like a business. After all you are now in business, the business of making money. Run your business so that it becomes a cycle that will continually grow more money.

There are always opportunities to grow your wealth. You can never learn too much and you will never know it all. Make it a habit to read magazines and books on investing and creating wealth. The more knowledge you gain will open paths to higher paying ventures.

You will find yourself willing to take more risks all while watching your profits grow. As you have learned creating a continuous flow of money takes proper planning, time, research and a lot of patience and discipline. However, the result of having a surplus of money coming in will serve as an opportunity for you to be able to enjoy more things in life. You will soon find that all the energy you put into increasing your wealth was well worth it in the end.

5.7 Pass It On

And finally pass it on! Teach your kids everything you have learned. Set up savings accounts for them and give them opportunities to make money so they can save money. Educate them on the correct practices of creating financial stability so they won't have to go through the pitfalls you went through. If you don't have kids pass this knowledge on to your friends and family. There is always someone who is secretly waiting for the insight on how to get out of his or her financial dilemma. You could be their help.

It's exciting that you have decided to change your life for the better and with all of your hard work and dedication you can rest assured that you will reach every goal you set for yourself.

Every milestone you cross will be another lesson learned. I can give you the knowledge you need to succeed now it's up to you to make it work.

I've Had My Turn Now It's Your Turn!

"If we had no winter, the spring would not be so pleasant: if we did not sometimes taste of adversity, prosperity would not be so welcome."
-Anne Bradstreet

I have taken the steps I used to create financial abundance for myself and have whole-heartedly given them to you. Every piece of advice here is what I gained from countless hours of research. It afforded me the ability to live a stress free life no longer worried about how I'm going to pay present or future bills. My only concern is creating more wealth, abundance and happiness. I pressed through the challenges and applied everything I learned to my stressful situation only to come out on top.

I know there was a lot of information presented to you here and you may feel like you still have a lot to do but it will prove it's weight in gold in the end.

Once you get started you will also notice your interest for more and more knowledge will be peaked and you will be willingly surfing the web and buying even more books on financial topics that can help you along the way.

I promise you once you really dedicate yourself to making your situation better and really focus and start doing the suggested exercises in this book you will see results and with those results will come gratification and a desire to do more so that you can see even bigger changes

None of the wealthy investors you see on television and the Internet became wealthy overnight. They had to put their time in and work their way to the top. It's the way of the world. Just as you can't plant a seed one day and expect to wake up the next morning only to see the flower has blossomed; you can't wish you had more money only to wake up and find it in your bank account.

Just as you will water the planted seed and check on it everyday until it has grown into a flower; you will do the same when working towards your forest of wealth. You will plant the seed of research and knowledge, water it with determination and discipline and watch it grow into multitudes with persistence and dedication. It is possible to achieve your financial dreams and now that you have been given the information to build a strong foundation there isn't any excuse not to do it! What's our favorite word??

COMMIT, COMMIT, COMMIT!

With that commitment and drive, you will be walking through your forest of money trees, happiness and abundance in no time.

Useful Information

Adjusting Your Thinking
(Part One: Page 10)
"The Science of Getting Rich"
Wallace D. Wattles

Debt Consolidation Guide
(Part Three: Page 50)
www.newcreditdebtconsolidation.com

Pro's And Cons Of Bankruptcy
(Part Three: Page 50)
www.consumeraffairs.com

Credit Repair
(Part Three: Page 50)
www.jdsrecoveries.com

Money Management Tools

(Part Three: Page 56)

www.quicken.intuit.com

Real Estate Investing

(Part Four: Page 64)

"The Beginners Guide To Real Estate Investing"

Gary W. Eldred, PhD

Financial Advisor Search

(Part Five: Page 105)

www.PaladinRegistry.com